THE
POWER
OF A
FIRST
STEP

Ignite Your Journey to Success and Fulfillment

JOHNATHAN RIVERS

MAROBOOKS PUBLISHING

ACKNOWLEDGMENTS

Writing a book like "The Power of a First Step: Ignite Your Journey to Success and Fulfillment" requires more than just determination and caffeine—it takes a village of incredible individuals who have supported, encouraged, and laughed along with me on this wild adventure. So, without further ado, here's my shout-out to the superheroes that made this book possible:

To my family, who managed to keep their eye rolls to a minimum every time I rambled on about my latest chapter or got lost in a sea of research papers—thank you for your unwavering patience and pretending to understand what I was talking about.

To my friends, the true MVPs who never failed to provide much-needed distractions, hilarious anecdotes, and occasional dance parties when writer's block threatened to take over my life. Your comedic relief and unwavering support made this journey all the more enjoyable. A massive thank you to, Dr. H. K. Dobson the grammar guru and keeper of the Oxford comma, for transforming my messy drafts into coherent prose. You've saved me from countless embarrassing typos and turned my words into something worth reading. I owe you more cups of coffee than I can count.

To my mentors, the wise sages who imparted their knowledge and shared their experiences, often with a side of quirky anecdotes and dad jokes. You've helped shape my perspective and shown me that learning can be both enlightening and entertaining.

A heartfelt thanks to all the readers and supporters of my work. Your enthusiasm, kind words, and willingness to dive into the weird and wonderful world of self-help books have motivated me to keep writing and sharing my ideas. You're the reason I continue to put words on paper.

And lastly, to all the brave souls who have taken their first steps towards their dreams, stumbling and tripping along the way but never losing sight of the finish line—I am constantly inspired by your resilience and unwavering determination. Thank you for reminding me of the power that lies within that initial leap.

To each and every one of you, whether you provided feedback, encouragement, or simply a good laugh, please know that your presence in my life and in the creation of this book has made all the difference.

With heartfelt appreciation, laughter, and a sprinkle of absurdity,

Johnathan Rivers.

CONTENTS

INTRODUCTION

In a world brimming with dreams and aspirations, there exists a force so potent, so transformative, that it has the potential to reshape destinies and ignite the spark of greatness within each of us. That force is none other than the power of a first step.

Imagine for a moment the exhilaration that surges through your veins as you summon the courage to take that decisive leap forward, shattering the chains of doubt and uncertainty that have held you back for far too long. Envision the rush of emotions as you embrace change and venture into the unknown, armed with nothing but a steadfast determination to fulfill your dreams.

"The Power of a First Step" is an invitation—an invitation to unleash your true potential, to transcend the boundaries of your comfort zone, and to embark on a remarkable journey of self-discovery, growth, and ultimate success. Within the pages of this book, you will find the guidance and inspiration needed to propel you forward, to make that all-important first step toward a life of fulfillment and purpose.

This book is not a mere collection of empty motivational clichés or unrealistic promises of instant success. Instead, it is a heartfelt exploration of the profound impact that one courageous act—the first step—can have on our lives. It delves deep into the stories of those who dared to dream, who embraced their passions, and who dared to take that crucial leap of faith.

Their stories serve as beacons of hope, illuminating the path that lies ahead and showcasing the extraordinary heights that can be reached by simply mustering the strength to begin.

As you navigate through the chapters of this book, you will discover the secrets behind the power of a first step. You will learn how to identify and overcome the paralyzing grip of fear and self-doubt that often holds us back from realizing our true potential. You will uncover the importance of setting clear goals, cultivating resilience, and maintaining unwavering determination even in the face of adversity.

But most importantly, "The Power of a First Step" is a call to action. It urges you to silence the voice of hesitation, to cast aside the shackles of complacency, and to embrace the transformative force that resides within you.

It provides practical exercises, thought-provoking questions, and actionable steps that will empower you to craft a roadmap to success—one step at a time.

The journey ahead will not be without challenges or setbacks. It will demand dedication, perseverance, and a steadfast belief in your own abilities. But with each turning page, I invite you to immerse yourself in the stories, insights, and strategies presented in this book. Allow them to kindle a flame within your soul, to ignite the passion that lies dormant, and to awaken the boundless potential that is uniquely yours.

Embrace the power of a first step. Embrace the courage to pursue your dreams. Embrace the extraordinary life that awaits you. The journey begins now. Are you ready to take that first step?

PART ONE: UNLOCKING

YOUR POTENTIAL

CHAPTER 1: THE FIRST STEP: A CATALYST FOR TRANSFORMATION

In the grand tapestry of life, there exists a pivotal moment that has the power to alter our trajectory, to set in motion a series of events that can lead to remarkable transformation. This moment is the first step—the moment when we summon the courage to venture into the unknown and embark on a path that holds the promise of fulfillment, success, and self-discovery.

"The First Step: A Catalyst for Transformation" explores the profound impact that taking that initial leap of faith can have on our lives. It explores the depths of human nature, uncovering the reasons why so many of us remain stagnant, trapped in the confines of our comfort zones, and hesitant to embrace change. Within this chapter, you will be introduced to the concept of the first step as a catalyst for transformation. You will gain a deeper understanding of the fears, doubts, and self-imposed limitations that often hold us back from pursuing our dreams. Through relatable anecdotes and insightful analysis, you will discover that true growth lies just beyond the threshold of our comfort.

As you embark on this journey of self-discovery, you will learn strategies to overcome fear and self-doubt, to silence the negative voices that seek to diminish your potential, and to cultivate the courage needed to take that all-important first step. You will be inspired by the stories of individuals who defied the odds, faced their fears head-on, and, in doing so, unleashed their true potential.

This chapter also highlights the importance of embracing change and the unknown. It invites you to recognize that the comfort of familiarity can often be a hindrance to progress and that by stepping outside of your comfort zone, you open yourself up to a world of possibilities. You will learn how to develop a mindset that welcomes change as an opportunity for growth and transformation, rather than a source of fear and resistance."The First Step: A Catalyst for Transformation" is an invitation to liberate oneself from the constraints of complacency, to question the prevailing norms, and to embark on a transformative expedition of self-exploration and growth. It encourages you to confront the barriers that have held you back and to embrace the untapped potential that lies within you.

As you absorb the wisdom contained within this chapter, reflect on your own life and consider the dreams and aspirations that have been simmering within your heart. What is the first step that will set you on a path towards the life you envision? What fears and doubts have held you back, and how can you overcome them? With each passing page, let the power of the first step stir within you a renewed sense of purpose, igniting the flame of transformation that will propel you towards a future filled with possibility and fulfillment.

Are you ready to take that first step?

UNDERSTANDING THE PROFOUND IMPACT OF TAKING THE FIRST STEP

In the grand tapestry of life, there exists a powerful truth: the first step is not just a physical act, but a profound catalyst for change. It is the pivotal moment that sets in motion a sequence of events, igniting a profound impact on our lives and the world around us. This section dives into the depths of understanding the profound impact of taking the first step, unraveling its transformative power and providing real-life examples that exemplify its potential.

Taking the first step is an act of courage that unleashes untapped potential within us. It pushes us beyond the confines of our comfort zones, opening doors to new opportunities and possibilities. Consider the aspiring artist who finally decides to showcase their work in a gallery. With that bold step, they invite the world to witness their creative expression, paving the way for recognition, growth, and the pursuit of their passion.

The first step has the remarkable ability to break through the barriers of fear and self-doubt that often hold us back. It challenges the limiting beliefs we hold about ourselves and propels us towards personal growth. Take, for instance, the individual who dreams of pursuing a career in public service but hesitates due to self-doubt. By taking the first step and applying for an internship or volunteering in a relevant organization, they overcome their insecurities, gain invaluable experience, and ultimately find themselves making a positive impact in the lives of others.

Every journey begins with a single step, and that first step creates a powerful momentum that propels us forward. Each subsequent step becomes easier as we build confidence, learn from our experiences, and adapt along the way. Consider the entrepreneur who takes the leap of faith to launch their start-up. With each milestone achieved, each customer acquired, and each obstacle overcome, their momentum grows, fueling their passion and driving them closer to success.

Understanding the profound impact of taking the first step requires a shift in mindset—a recognition that small actions can yield tremendous results. It empowers us to embrace our dreams, conquer our fears, and embark on a journey of growth and self-actualization. The above mentioned real-life examples demonstrate the transformative power of that initial act, inspiring us to seize opportunities, break through barriers, and create a ripple effect of positive change.

As you reflect on your own life, consider the dreams and aspirations that have been waiting to be realized. What is the first step that will set your journey in motion? Embrace the profound impact it can have and find the courage to take that decisive leap forward. The world eagerly awaits the transformative power that lies within you.

Fear and self-doubt are formidable barriers that hinder our progress and keep us from reaching our full potential. However, in the face of these challenges, the power of taking the first step becomes even more significant. This chapter delves into the depths of overcoming fear and self-doubt, providing insights and strategies to empower you to embrace courage, conquer your inner demons, and take that vital first step towards realizing your dreams.

Understanding Fear and Self-Doubt: Fear and self-doubt are natural aspects of the human experience. They stem from our desire for security and our fear of failure or judgment. However, when left unchecked, they can paralyze us and prevent us from pursuing our passions. By understanding the roots of fear and self-doubt, we can begin to dismantle their power and regain control over our lives.

Embracing the Growth Mindset: A key strategy in overcoming fear and self-doubt is cultivating a growth mindset. Embrace the belief that challenges and setbacks are opportunities for growth rather than indicators of failure. Adopt a mindset that views failures as valuable lessons, leading to personal and professional development. With this mindset, you can approach your fears and self-doubts as stepping stones towards success, resilience, and self-discovery.

Reframing Limiting Beliefs: Our beliefs shape our reality, including the way we perceive ourselves and our abilities. Often, fear and self-doubt arise from limiting beliefs we hold about our potential or worthiness. By challenging and reframing these beliefs, we can create a new narrative that empowers us. Replace self-defeating thoughts with positive affirmations and visualize your success. Over time, you will strengthen your belief in your capabilities and develop the confidence needed to overcome fear and self-doubt.

Taking Incremental Steps: Overcoming fear and self-doubt doesn't happen overnight. It requires taking small, manageable steps towards your goals.

Break down your aspirations into smaller tasks or milestones that feel less overwhelming. Each step taken builds momentum, boosts confidence, and gradually diminishes the power of fear and self-doubt. Celebrate your progress, no matter how small, and use it as motivation to continue moving forward.

Illustrative Instances: Consider the aspiring public speaker who feared being judged and criticized. Through consistent practice, stepping out of their comfort zone to speak at smaller events, and seeking constructive feedback, they gradually silenced their self-doubt and became a confident, inspiring communicator. Another example is the individual who longed to change careers but was held back by the fear of starting from scratch. By taking calculated risks, pursuing further education or training, and seeking guidance from mentors, they overcame their doubts and successfully transitioned into a fulfilling new career.

Overcoming fear and self-doubt is a vital step on the journey towards success and personal fulfillment. By understanding the nature of these challenges, adopting a growth mindset, reframing limiting beliefs, and taking incremental steps, you can break free from their grip. Realize that fear and self-doubt are conquerable adversaries, and the power of the first step is the key to unlocking your potential.

While treading your unique journey, always bear in mind that courage is not the absence of fear, but rather the boldness to take action despite its presence. Embrace the challenges, doubts, and fears that arise, knowing that they are stepping stones towards growth. Harness the power within you, overcome your inner barriers, and take that crucial first step towards a life filled with achievement, joy, and self-empowerment. As you reflect on your own life, consider the dreams and aspirations that have been waiting to be realized. What is the first step that will set your journey in motion? Embrace the profound impact it can have and find the courage to take that decisive leap forward. The world eagerly awaits the transformative power that lies within you.

Change is an inescapable and perpetual facet of existence. It is through change that we grow, learn, and evolve. However, embracing change and venturing into the unknown can be daunting. We will examine the transformative power of embracing change and the unknown. We will uncover the opportunities that lie within the uncharted territory, and discover how taking the first step towards the unknown can lead to personal and professional breakthroughs.

The unknown can be intimidating, as it represents a departure from our familiar routines and comfort zones. However, it is within this realm of uncertainty that true growth and transformation occur. By embracing the unknown, we open ourselves up to new possibilities, experiences, and perspectives. It is a reminder that life's greatest adventures and discoveries often await us on the other side of fear.

Change requires adaptability, resilience, and a willingness to let go of old ways. It is in the face of change that we discover our true capacity for growth. Consider the individual who finds themselves unexpectedly laid off from a long-standing job. Although initially unsettling, this change presents an opportunity to reassess their career goals, learn new skills, and explore uncharted professional territories. By embracing the change, they may discover a more fulfilling and rewarding path than they had ever imagined.

Embracing change and the unknown requires us to step outside our comfort zones. It demands that we confront our fears, challenge our assumptions, and be open to new experiences. By leaning into discomfort, we expand our horizons and develop a resilience that enables us to thrive in an ever-changing world. The first step into the unknown becomes a powerful act of self-discovery, pushing the boundaries of what we thought possible.

Within change and the unknown lie hidden opportunities. It is by taking the first step into uncharted territory that we uncover new paths, untapped potential, and unforeseen connections. Consider the entrepreneur who decides to pivot their business in response to market trends. By embracing the change, they may discover a previously untapped market niche or develop innovative solutions that catapult their venture to new heights.

Embracing change and the unknown has a transformative power. Think of the individual who relocates to a foreign country, leaving behind their familiar surroundings and social networks. Despite the initial challenges, they embrace the change as an opportunity for personal growth, cultural immersion, and broadening their perspectives. Through their experiences, they develop resilience, adaptability, and a global mindset.

Embracing change and the unknown is a testament to our willingness to grow and evolve. It is an acknowledgement that life's greatest rewards often lie beyond our comfort zones. By taking the first step into uncharted territory, we embark on a journey of self-discovery, personal growth, and boundless possibilities. Realize that change is not a threat, but a catalyst for transformation. Embrace the unknown with an open heart and a curious mind, and witness the power that lies within the first step towards change and the unexplored

CHAPTER 2: IGNITING YOUR PASSION

Passion is the fuel that propels us forward on our journey towards success and fulfillment. It is the fire within us that ignites our creativity, drive, and determination. In this chapter, we delve into the power of igniting your passion and explore how taking the first step towards pursuing your true calling can set the stage for a remarkable and meaningful journey. Many individuals go through life without truly discovering their passion. They may find themselves stuck in monotonous routine or pursuing careers that do not align with their true interests and talents. However, by embarking on a journey of self-discovery and reflection, we can uncover our passions, those activities that bring us joy, excitement, and a deep sense of purpose. Taking the first step towards exploring and nurturing these passions is the key to unlocking our potential and finding fulfillment.

Passion is not only about what brings us joy but also about aligning our actions with our core values. When our passion aligns with our values, we experience a sense of integrity and authenticity. It becomes a driving force that fuels our determination to make a positive impact in the world. By taking the first step towards aligning our passions with our values, we create a solid foundation for success and fulfillment.

While passion can ignite a fire within us, resistance often tries to extinguish it. Resistance comes in various forms, such as self-doubt, fear of failure, or external discouragement. Taking the first step towards pursuing our passions requires us to overcome these obstacles and persevere. It demands that we cultivate resilience, surround ourselves with supportive individuals, and cultivate a mindset that embraces challenges as opportunities for growth. Passion without action remains dormant. To fully harness the power of your passion, you must take the first step towards translating it into tangible actions. This could involve acquiring new skills, seeking mentors or role models, or diving into projects or initiatives that align with your passion. By embracing the unknown and stepping outside your comfort zone, you breathe life into your passion, fueling your journey towards success and fulfillment.

Igniting your passion is the catalyst that sets your

journey towards success and fulfillment in motion. By taking the first step towards discovering and nurturing your passions, aligning them with your values, and turning them into actionable steps, you unleash your true potential and embark on a transformative path. Realize that passion is not something to be pursued passively; it requires your active engagement and commitment. Embrace the power of your passions, take that first step, and watch as your journey unfolds with purpose, meaning, and the joy of pursuing what truly sets your soul on fire.

Within each of us lies a unique combination of talents, interests, and desires waiting to be discovered. We will explore how taking the first step towards this self-exploration can unlock a profound sense of meaning, fulfillment, and direction in your life.

Discovering your true passions and purpose is an inward quest, a journey of self-exploration and reflection. It requires a willingness to delve deep into your interests, values, and experiences to unearth the activities and pursuits that ignite a genuine sense of joy and purpose within you. Taking the first step towards self-discovery involves creating space for introspection, engaging in activities that resonate with your innermost desires, and paying attention to the moments that truly light you up.

Each of us possesses a unique set of talents and strengths that can guide us towards our true passions and purpose. These talents may come naturally to us or require development and refinement over time. Taking the first step towards recognizing and nurturing your talents involves embracing self-awareness, seeking feedback from others, and engaging in activities that allow your strengths to shine. By recognizing and harnessing your unique talents, you lay the foundation for a fulfilling and purpose-driven life.

Understanding your core values is a vital step in discovering your true passions and purpose. Values serve as guiding principles that shape your beliefs, choices, and actions. Taking the first step towards aligning your passions with your values involves exploring what truly matters to you, examining the impact you wish to have on the world, and seeking opportunities that resonate with your core values. When your passions align with your values, you embark on a path that feels authentic and meaningful, empowering you to make a difference in your own life and the lives of others.

Purpose is the driving force that infuses your life with meaning and fulfillment. It is the deep sense of significance and contribution that arises when your passions align with a larger vision or mission. Taking the first step towards unleashing the power of purpose involves identifying the ways in which your passions can create a positive impact in the world. It requires a commitment to continuously seek opportunities to align your actions with your purpose, whether through your career, creative pursuits, relationships, or community involvement.

Taking the first step towards discovering your true passions and purpose is a catalyst for profound transformation.

It signifies a commitment to self-growth, a willingness to explore the unknown, and a readiness to embrace change. Each step taken on this journey brings you closer to uncovering your authentic self, allowing you to live a life that is aligned with your deepest desires and values. The first step creates momentum, propelling you towards new opportunities, connections, and experiences that further illuminate your path.

As you embark on the journey of discovering your true passions and purpose, you may be surprised by the profound impact it has on every aspect of your life. It affects your sense of fulfillment, your relationships, your career choices, and your overall well-being. By taking the first step, you open yourself up to a world of possibilities, a life filled with purpose, and the opportunity to make a lasting impact on the world around you.

Discovering your true passions and purpose is a transformative and ongoing journey. By taking the first step towards self-discovery, recognizing your unique talents, aligning with your values, and embracing your purpose, you unlock a profound sense of meaning, joy, and fulfillment in your life. Remember that the first step is not only significant in itself, but it also sets in motion a series of transformative events. It signifies our willingness to embrace change, unlocks our potential, and inspires others. By taking that initial leap, we set ourselves on a trajectory of growth and open doors to new opportunities and experiences. It is the start of a remarkable journey, where each subsequent step takes us further along the path of success and fulfillment.

CULTIVATING ENTHUSIASM AND MOTIVATION

Enthusiasm and motivation are the driving forces that propel us forward on the path to success and fulfillment. In this chapter, we explore the power of cultivating enthusiasm and motivation and how taking the first step plays a pivotal role in nurturing these essential qualities. We will explore strategies for igniting and sustaining enthusiasm, overcoming obstacles, and maintaining a strong sense of motivation throughout your journey.

Enthusiasm is the spark that ignites your passion, fuels your energy, and infuses joy into your pursuits. It is a contagious force that radiates from within and attracts opportunities and positive experiences. Taking the first step towards your goals with enthusiasm creates a ripple effect, inspiring others and creating a positive environment for growth and achievement.

To cultivate and sustain enthusiasm, it is crucial to engage in activities and pursuits that align with your passions and values. Taking the first step towards these endeavors creates a sense of purpose and excitement. Additionally, surrounding yourself with like-minded individuals, seeking out mentors and role models, and celebrating small wins along the way can further nurture your enthusiasm. Embrace challenges as opportunities for growth, and maintain a mindset of curiosity and continuous learning.

Obstacles and setbacks are inevitable on any journey. However, maintaining enthusiasm and motivation requires resilience and a proactive approach to overcoming these challenges. Taking the first step in the face of adversity is an act of determination and perseverance. It is an acknowledgment that obstacles are merely temporary roadblocks and opportunities for growth. By reframing setbacks as learning experiences and seeking solutions rather than dwelling on problems, you can maintain your enthusiasm and keep your motivation intact.

Meaningful goals serve as the driving force behind sustained motivation. Taking the first step towards setting these goals involves clarity and intention. By aligning your goals with your passions, values, and long-term vision, you create a strong foundation for motivation. Divide your goals into attainable milestones and commemorate every accomplishment on your journey. This incremental progress will fuel your motivation and inspire you to keep taking further steps towards success.

Accountability and support play a crucial role in maintaining motivation. Sharing your goals and progress with trusted friends, family, or mentors can provide a sense of external accountability. Seek out individuals who believe in your potential and can provide guidance and encouragement. Joining communities or groups with shared interests can also foster a sense of support and motivation. The collective energy and shared experiences can inspire you to stay focused and committed to your journey.

As you take the first step and continue to progress towards your goals, it is essential to celebrate your achievements, no matter how small. Acknowledge the effort, dedication, and growth you have demonstrated along the way. Celebrating milestones and victories boosts your motivation and reinforces the belief that you are capable of achieving even more. Use these celebrations as fuel to propel you forward on your journey.

Cultivating enthusiasm and motivation is a dynamic process that requires continuous nurturing and self-reflection. By taking the first step towards your goals with enthusiasm, overcoming obstacles with resilience, setting meaningful goals, seeking accountability and support, and celebrating your progress, you create a powerful cycle of motivation. Embrace the journey, stay connected to your passions, and let your enthusiasm be the driving force that propels you towards success and fulfilment.

Passion is a powerful force that can drive us towards our aspirations and dreams. However, without channeling that passion towards meaningful goals, it can dissipate and lose its impact. In this chapter, we explore the significance of directing our passion towards purposeful objectives and how taking the first step plays a pivotal role in this process. We delve into strategies for setting meaningful goals, maintaining focus, and leveraging passion to achieve remarkable outcomes.

Defining Meaningful Goals: Meaningful goals are those that align with our passions, values, and long-term vision. They possess a sense of purpose and significance that fuels our drive and commitment. Taking the first step towards defining meaningful goals requires self-reflection, introspection, and a clear understanding of what truly matters to us. By identifying goals that resonate with our passion, we create a powerful connection that drives us forward on our journey.

Setting SMART Goals: Once we have identified our meaningful goals, it is crucial to structure them in a way that makes them achievable and actionable. The SMART (Specific, Measurable, Attainable, Relevant, Time-bound) framework provides a valuable framework for goal setting. By taking the first step towards setting SMART goals, we create clarity and focus, making it easier to channel our passion towards their attainment. Specificity and measurability allow us to track progress, while attainability and relevance ensure that our goals align with our capabilities and aspirations. Setting deadlines adds a sense of urgency and commitment, motivating us to take consistent action.

Maintaining Focus and Momentum: Passion is a powerful force, but without focus, it can scatter our efforts and hinder progress. Taking the first step towards maintaining focus involves eliminating distractions, establishing priorities, and cultivating discipline. By developing habits that align with our goals and dedicating regular time and energy towards their pursuit, we harness the full potential of our passion. Additionally, regularly revisiting our goals and visualizing their attainment helps reignite our passion and keeps us motivated and on track.

Translating Passion into Action: Passion alone is not enough to achieve our goals; it must be coupled with decisive action. Taking the first step towards translating our passion into action involves breaking down our goals into manageable tasks and creating a plan of action. Each step we take brings us closer to our aspirations, providing a sense of fulfillment and progress. By leveraging our passion as a driving force, we find the energy, determination, and resilience necessary to overcome obstacles and push through challenges on our path towards success.

Embracing Adaptability and Growth: As we channel our passion towards meaningful goals, it is essential to embrace adaptability and growth. The journey towards our goals is rarely linear, and unexpected twists and turns may arise. Taking the first step towards embracing adaptability involves maintaining an open mindset, being willing to learn from setbacks, and making necessary adjustments along the way. Our passion acts as a guiding light, guiding us through uncertainty and motivating us to explore new avenues and possibilities.

Realizing the Transformative Power: When we channel our passion towards meaningful goals, we tap into a transformative power within ourselves. Taking the first step towards aligning our passion with purposeful objectives unleashes our potential and propels us towards extraordinary achievements. Our passion becomes the driving force that pushes us beyond our comfort zones, fuels our resilience, and allows us to surpass our own expectations. The impact we make through the pursuit of our goals extends far beyond our individual selves, inspiring and influencing those around us.

Channeling our passion towards meaningful goals is a transformative process that empowers us to create a lasting impact. By taking the first step towards setting meaningful goals, maintaining focus, translating passion into action, embracing adaptability, and recognizing the transformative power within us, we unlock the pathway to success and fulfilment.

CHAPTER 3: SETTING GOALS FOR SUCCESS

Goals are the compass that guides us on our journey to success and fulfillment. In this chapter, we explore the significance of setting goals and how they serve as the roadmap for our achievements. We will take a look into the process of setting effective and inspiring goals, understanding the different types of goals, and the transformative impact of taking the first step towards their realization. Setting goals is the foundation for progress and growth. It allows us to define our aspirations, clarify our direction, and focus our efforts. Goals provide us with a sense of purpose and motivation, propelling us forward even in the face of challenges. Taking the first step towards setting goals is an act of intention, signaling our commitment to personal and professional development.

There are different types of goals that we can set to encompass various areas of our lives. They can be categorized into short-term, medium-term, and long-term goals. Short-term goals provide immediate targets and allow us to experience a sense of accomplishment in the near future. Medium-term goals span a few months to a year and help us achieve significant milestones. Long-term goals are ambitious and encompass our vision for the future, guiding our overall life direction. By setting a combination of these goals, we create a well-rounded framework for success.

Effective goals are those that are specific, measurable, attainable, relevant, and time-bound (SMART). Taking the first step towards creating effective goals involves being clear and precise in defining what we want to achieve. By making our goals measurable, we can track progress and evaluate success. It is important to ensure that our goals are realistic and attainable, considering our capabilities and available resources. Relevance to our overall vision and aspirations is crucial, and setting deadlines adds a sense of urgency and accountability.

Once we have set our goals, it is powerful to visualize their attainment and affirm their achievement. Taking the first step towards visualizing our goals involves creating vivid mental images of ourselves successfully accomplishing our objectives. Visualization helps to reinforce our motivation, clarify our intentions, and strengthen our belief in our capabilities. Affirmations are positive statements that we repeat to ourselves, reinforcing our confidence and conviction in achieving our goals. By visualizing and affirming our goals, we align our subconscious mind with our conscious intentions, creating a powerful mindset for success.

Goals can often seem overwhelming, especially when they are ambitious or long-term in nature. To make them more manageable, it is essential to break them down into smaller, actionable steps. Taking the first step towards breaking goals into actionable steps involves identifying the specific actions or milestones required to progress towards our goals. By focusing on these smaller steps, we can maintain momentum, track progress, and celebrate achievements along the way. Breaking goals into actionable steps makes them more tangible and increases our likelihood of success.

The pursuit of goals is not always a smooth journey. Challenges, setbacks, and unexpected circumstances are inevitable. Taking the first step towards achieving our goals involves recognizing that obstacles are opportunities for growth and learning. When confronted with obstacles, maintaining resilience and flexibility is paramount. By adjusting our course, seeking alternative strategies, and learning from setbacks, we can overcome obstacles and keep moving forward towards our goals.

As we make progress towards our goals, it is crucial

to celebrate milestones and successes along the way. Taking the first step towards celebrating achievements is an act of self-recognition and appreciation. By acknowledging our efforts and the progress we have made, we cultivate a positive mindset and maintain motivation. Celebrating milestones also provides an opportunity to reflect on our journey, reassess our goals, and set new targets

THE IMPORTANCE OF SETTING CLEAR AND ACHIEVABLE GOALS

Setting clear and achievable goals is crucial for success and personal fulfillment. In this section, we will explore the significance of setting clear and achievable goals and how they can propel us forward on our journey.

Clarity of Direction: Clear goals provide a roadmap for our actions and decisions. When we have a clear vision of what we want to achieve, we can align our efforts and resources towards that specific direction. Clarity eliminates ambiguity and allows us to focus our time and energy on activities that contribute to the realization of our goals.

Motivation and Commitment: Clear goals ignite our motivation and commitment. When we have a well-defined objective in mind, we are more likely to stay motivated and dedicated to its attainment. Clear goals create a sense of purpose and excitement, fueling our enthusiasm and drive. They act as a constant reminder of what we are working towards, helping us push through challenges and stay focused.

Measurement and Progress Tracking: Clear goals are measurable, which means we can track our progress and evaluate our performance. When we set specific targets, we can assess how far we have come and how much further we need to go. This measurement provides a sense of achievement and allows us to make adjustments and improvements along the way. Clear goals enable us to monitor our progress effectively and make necessary changes if we find ourselves off track.

Increased Confidence and Self-Belief: Achieving clear and achievable goals enhances our confidence and self-belief. When we set goals that are within our reach, we experience a sense of accomplishment with each milestone we reach. This incremental success boosts our self-esteem and reinforces the belief that we are capable of achieving even more. As we consistently meet our goals, our confidence grows, empowering us to set higher aspirations and tackle more significant challenges.

Focus and Prioritization: Clear goals help us prioritize our efforts and avoid distractions. With a clear understanding of what we want to achieve, we can eliminate non-essential tasks and concentrate on activities that directly contribute to our goals. Setting clear goals allows us to allocate our time, resources, and energy efficiently, ensuring that we make progress towards our objectives without getting sidetracked by unrelated or less important endeavors.

Accountability and Commitment: Clear goals hold us accountable for our actions. When we clearly define our goals, we create a sense of responsibility to follow through and take the necessary steps towards their accomplishment. The clarity of our goals enables us to set specific deadlines and milestones, which adds a layer of accountability to our journey. This accountability ensures that we remain committed and take consistent action towards our goals.

Adaptability and Flexibility: While setting clear goals is important, it is equally essential to remain adaptable and flexible in our approach. Life is full of uncertainties, and circumstances may undergo transformations throughout the journey. Clear goals, coupled with flexibility, allow us to adjust our strategies and adapt to new situations without losing sight of our ultimate objectives. Flexibility enables us to embrace opportunities, navigate challenges, and make necessary revisions to our goals while maintaining clarity and focus.

In summary, setting clear and achievable goals is a fundamental aspect of success and personal growth. Clear goals provide us with direction, motivation, and a framework for progress. They enhance our confidence, focus our efforts, and hold us accountable for our actions. By setting clear and achievable goals, we empower ourselves to reach our full potential and lead a purpose-driven life.

CREATING A VISION FOR YOUR FUTURE

A powerful and transformative journey begins with a clear vision of the future you desire. In this subsection, we explore the importance of creating a vision for your future and how it acts as a guiding light on your path to success and fulfillment. We will explore the process of envisioning your ideal future, the benefits it brings, and the impact it has on taking that crucial first step towards turning your dreams into reality.

A vision is a mental picture of the future you aspire to create. It is a representation of your deepest desires, values, and aspirations. When you create a vision for your future, you give shape and form to your dreams, making them more tangible and compelling. A powerful vision acts as a beacon, guiding your thoughts, decisions, and actions. It fuels your motivation, ignites your passion, and provides a sense of purpose and direction.

To create a vision for your future, it requires introspection, imagination, and clarity. Begin by reflecting on what truly matters to you and what you want to achieve in different areas of your life, such as career, relationships, personal growth, and contribution to society. Visualize your ideal future with vivid detail, imagining how it would feel, look, and sound. Embrace the possibilities and allow yourself to dream without limitations. As you delve deeper into envisioning your ideal future, you gain a deeper understanding of what drives and inspires you.

The Benefits of Creating a Vision: Creating a vision for your future offers numerous benefits that propel you towards success and fulfillment:

Clarity and Focus: A clear vision provides clarity and focus, helping you prioritize your efforts and make informed decisions. It serves as a compass, guiding you towards activities and opportunities that align with your vision while filtering out distractions that may derail your progress.

Motivation and Resilience: A compelling vision fuels your motivation and strengthens your resilience. When faced with challenges or setbacks, your vision reminds you of the greater purpose and keeps you motivated to overcome obstacles and persevere on your journey.

Alignment with Values: A well-defined vision ensures alignment with your core values and beliefs. It allows you to live authentically, making choices and taking actions that resonate with your deepest principles. This alignment brings a sense of integrity and harmony to your life.

Setting Meaningful Goals: A vision provides a framework for setting meaningful goals. It helps you identify the milestones and achievements that will contribute to the realization of your vision. With a clear vision, you can set specific, measurable, and purposeful goals that align with your desired future.

Once you have created a vision for your future, the power lies in taking that critical first step towards its realization. This step signifies your commitment and belief in the vision you have crafted. It may involve stepping out of your comfort zone, embracing uncertainty, and taking calculated risks. The first step sets in motion a chain of actions and opportunities that move you closer to your vision, building momentum and propelling you forward.

Creating a vision for your future is a transformative process that shapes your journey towards success and fulfillment. It provides a roadmap, fuels your motivation, and guides your actions. By envisioning your ideal future and taking that all-important first step, you embark on a remarkable adventure, armed with purpose, passion, and the power to turn your dreams into reality.

DEVELOPING AN EFFECTIVE GOAL-SETTING STRATEGY

Goal setting is a powerful tool that propels us towards success and fulfillment. Within this section, we explore the significance of crafting an effective goal-setting strategy and its profound influence on our personal journey. We explore the key components of a successful goal-setting process, techniques to enhance goal clarity and specificity, and methods to stay motivated and committed throughout the pursuit of our goals.

The Key Components of an Effective Goal-Setting Strategy:

Reflect on Your Values and Priorities: Before setting goals, it is essential to reflect on your values and priorities. Consider what truly matters to you and align your goals with your core beliefs. This ensures that your goals are meaningful and authentic, increasing your motivation and sense of fulfillment when you achieve them.

Be Specific and Measurable: Effective goals are specific and measurable. Clearly define what you want to accomplish and quantify your objectives whenever possible. Specific goals provide clarity and guide your actions, while measurable goals allow you to track progress and evaluate success along the way.

Set Realistic and Attainable Goals: While it is important to set ambitious goals, they should also be realistic and attainable. Assess your current capabilities, available resources, and time constraints. Setting goals that stretch your abilities without overwhelming you increases your chances of success and prevents discouragement.

Break Goals into Actionable Steps: To make your goals more manageable, break them down into actionable steps. Identify the specific tasks or milestones required to reach each goal. Breaking goals into smaller steps not only provides a clear roadmap but also allows you to celebrate incremental achievements, maintaining motivation throughout the journey.

Establish Deadlines and Timeframes: Setting deadlines and timeframes is crucial to creating a sense of urgency and accountability. Assign specific dates or timeframes to each goal and its corresponding action steps. Having a timeline helps you stay focused, avoid procrastination, and allocate your time and resources effectively.

Enhancing Goal Clarity and Specificity:

Visualization Techniques: Utilize visualization techniques to enhance goal clarity. Immerse yourself in a vivid visualization of attaining your goals, allowing your imagination to paint a vibrant picture of success. Engage all your senses, picturing how it feels, looks, and sounds. Visualization strengthens your belief in your ability to achieve your goals and enhances your motivation.

Journaling and Writing: Write down your goals in a journal or on paper. Describe them in detail, outlining the specific outcomes you desire. Writing clarifies your thoughts, reinforces your commitment, and acts as a reference point for tracking progress.

Staying Motivated and Committed:

Find Your Why: Understand the underlying reasons and motivations behind your goals. Reflect on how achieving them will improve your life or contribute to your personal growth. Connecting emotionally with your goals creates a deeper sense of purpose and commitment.

Regular Progress Assessment: Regularly assess your progress towards your goals. Celebrate milestones and accomplishments, reinforcing your motivation. If you encounter setbacks, learn from them and adjust your approach if needed. Recognize that setbacks are part of the journey and use them as opportunities for growth.

Accountability and Support: Share your goals with a trusted friend, mentor, or accountability partner. Regularly update them on your progress and seek their support and encouragement. Having someone to hold you accountable increases your commitment and helps you stay on track.

Developing an effective goal-setting strategy is instrumental in igniting your journey to success and fulfillment. By reflecting on your values, setting specific and measurable goals, breaking them into actionable steps, and staying motivated and committed, you create a powerful framework for achievement. Remember, the first step towards your goals is the catalyst for transformation, and with an effective goal-setting strategy, you set yourself up for an extraordinary journey of growth, accomplishment, and self-discovery.

PART TWO: OVERCOMING CHALLENGES

CHAPTER 4: BUILDING RESILIENCE

In this chapter, we explore the concept of resilience and its crucial role in our journey towards success and fulfillment. Resilience is the ability to bounce back from adversity, adapt to challenges, and persevere in the face of setbacks. We examine closely the importance of building resilience, strategies to cultivate resilience in our lives, and how resilience impacts our ability to take that crucial first step and navigate the inevitable obstacles that arise along our path.

Resilience is a fundamental quality that empowers us to overcome obstacles, learn from failures, and maintain our drive and determination. It acts as a shield against discouragement, self-doubt, and external setbacks that may threaten our progress. By building resilience, we enhance our ability to stay focused, motivated, and committed, even in the face of adversity.

Surrounding ourselves with a supportive network of family, friends, mentors, and like-minded individuals can significantly enhance our resilience. These individuals provide encouragement, guidance, and a safe space for us to express our challenges and seek support. Their presence reminds us that we are not alone in our journey and strengthens our ability to bounce back from setbacks.

Building resilience has a profound impact on our ability to take the first step towards our goals and dreams. When we are resilient, we are more willing to embrace uncertainty and step out of our comfort zones. We are better equipped to manage fear, self-doubt, and the potential for failure. Resilience empowers us to view the first step as anopportunity for growth and transformation, rather than a paralyzing barrier.

Furthermore, resilience ensures that setbacks and obstacles do not derail us from our path. Instead, they become learning experiences and opportunities for course correction. With resilience, we bounce back from failures, adapt our strategies, and remain committed to our journey despite the challenges we encounter. Building resilience is a vital component of our journey towards success and fulfillment.

By cultivating a resilient mindset, practicing self-compassion, nurturing a supportive network, and developing emotional intelligence, we strengthen our ability to overcome adversity and stay committed to our goals. Resilience empowers us to take that critical first step, navigate obstacles, and continue moving forward on our path, regardless of the challenges we face.

It is a valuable asset that ensures our journey is marked by resilience, perseverance, and ultimately, triumphs.

UNDERSTANDING THE ROLE OF RESIL-
IENCE IN OVERCOMING OBSTACLES

In this section, we thoroughly analyze the vital role that resilience plays in our ability to overcome obstacles on our journey towards success and fulfillment. Resilience is the inner strength that allows us to face challenges, bounce back from setbacks, and persevere in the face of adversity. By understanding the significance of resilience, we can harness its power to navigate obstacles effectively and continue moving forward with unwavering determination.

Resilience serves as a crucial asset in our pursuit of success and fulfillment. It empowers us to view obstacles not as insurmountable barriers, but as opportunities for growth and learning. Rather than succumbing to defeat or becoming discouraged, resilience fuels our determination to find alternative paths and solutions.

It enables us to maintain a positive mindset and a sense of hope, even in the face of the most daunting challenges. Resilience allows us to embrace change and navigate uncertainty with confidence. It provides the mental and emotional strength to adapt to new circumstances, adjust our strategies, and remain flexible in the face of unexpected turns. With resilience, we develop the resilience to step out of our comfort zones and take calculated risks, knowing that failure is merely a stepping stone towards success.

Resilience enables us to learn from setbacks rather than be defined by them. It encourages us to reflect on our experiences, extract valuable lessons, and integrate them into our future actions. Instead of being deterred by failure, resilient individuals use it as an opportunity for growth and self-improvement. They bounce back stronger, armed with newfound knowledge and a determination to persevere.

When confronted with obstacles, it is easy to lose focus and motivation. However, resilience serves as an anchor that keeps us grounded and driven towards our goals. It helps us maintain perspective, reminding us of the bigger picture and the reasons why we embarked on our journey in the first place. Resilience fuels our motivation, reignites our passion, and ensures that we stay committed, even when the path seems arduous. Resilience fosters the development of effective problem-solving skills. Instead of being overwhelmed by obstacles, resilient individuals approach them with a proactive mindset. They seek creative solutions, break down challenges into manageable steps, and engage in critical thinking. Resilience empowers us to approach obstacles with resourcefulness and tenacity, increasing our chances of finding innovative and effective solutions.

Understanding the role of resilience in overcoming obstacles is essential on our journey to success and fulfillment.

By cultivating resilience, we equip ourselves with the strength and determination to face challenges head-on.

Resilience empowers us to embrace change, learn from setbacks, maintain focus, and develop problem-solving skills.

It allows us to navigate obstacles with grace and fortitude, propelling us forward on our path

With resilience as our ally, no obstacle is insurmountable, and every challenge becomes an opportunity for growth and transformation.

DEVELOPING A RESILIENT MINDSET

We investigate in details the importance of cultivating a resilient mindset on our journey to success and fulfillment. A resilient mindset is the foundation upon which we build our ability to navigate challenges, setbacks, and uncertainties. By understanding the key elements of a resilient mindset and actively developing it, we can strengthen our capacity to overcome obstacles and persevere in the pursuit of our goals.

Embracing a Growth Mindset: A resilient mindset begins with embracing a growth mindset. This mindset is rooted in the belief that our abilities, intelligence, and talents can be developed through dedication, effort, and continuous learning.

By cultivating a growth mindset, we view challenges as opportunities for growth and see setbacks as temporary hurdles rather than permanent failures. This perspective allows us to approach obstacles with a sense of curiosity, resilience, and determination.

Cultivating Self-Awareness: Self-awareness is a vital component of a resilient mindset. It involves understanding our strengths, weaknesses, emotions, and thought patterns. By developing self-awareness, we can identify our triggers, recognize when we are becoming overwhelmed, and proactively take steps to manage stress and maintain emotional balance. Self-awareness enables us to respond to challenges with clarity and adaptability, rather than reacting impulsively or being consumed by negative emotions.

Practicing Adaptability: Adaptability is a hallmark of resilience. In an ever-changing world, being able to adjust our strategies, perspectives, and approaches is essential. Developing a resilient mindset involves embracing flexibility, being open to new ideas, and adapting to shifting circumstances. By cultivating adaptability, we become more adept at navigating uncertainties and bouncing back from unexpected challenges. We learn to see change as an opportunity for growth rather than a source of fear or resistance.

Fostering a Positive Outlook: A resilient mindset is nurtured by maintaining a positive outlook. While it is natural to experience moments of doubt, setbacks, and even failure, a resilient mindset allows us to reframe these experiences as opportunities for learning and personal growth.

By adopting a positive outlook, we focus on solutions, possibilities, and the lessons embedded within each challenge. A positive mindset strengthens our resilience, empowers us to persevere, and fuels our motivation to keep moving forward.

Cultivating Resilient Habits: Developing a resilient mindset requires consistent practice and the cultivation of resilient habits. These may include setting realistic goals, developing a support network, practicing self-care, and engaging in regular reflection and gratitude. Resilient habits serve as the building blocks of our mindset, reinforcing our resilience and enhancing our ability to face adversity head-on.

Developing a resilient mindset is a transformative endeavor that lays the groundwork for overcoming obstacles and achieving success and fulfillment. By embracing a growth mindset, cultivating self-awareness, practicing adaptability, fostering a positive outlook, and nurturing resilient habits, we fortify our mental and emotional strength.

A resilient mindset empowers us to face challenges with courage, bounce back from setbacks with resilience, and maintain unwavering determination on our journey.

With a resilient mindset as our foundation, we have the power to ignite our journey to success and fulfillment, confidently taking that all-important first step towards realizing our dreams.

Within this section, we probe intensively into a range of
strategies that empower individuals to effectively rebound
from setbacks and failures encountered on their path to
success and fulfillment. By embracing and implementing
these strategies, individuals can enhance their ability to
navigate challenges, recover from setbacks, and emerge
stronger and more determined to continue progressing towards their goals. Setbacks and failures are inevitable
parts of any pursuit, but how we respond to them can
make all the difference. By understanding and implementing these strategies, we can navigate setbacks with resilience, learn from failures, and emerge stronger and more
determined to move forward.

Embrace a Growth Mindset: A growth mindset is
essential when bouncing back from setbacks and failures.
Embrace the belief that setbacks are opportunities for
growth and learning, rather than permanent roadblocks.
Adopt a perspective that failure is not the end, but a stepping stone toward success. By viewing setbacks as learning experiences, you can extract valuable lessons, adjust
your approach, and continue progressing on your journey.

Practice Self-Compassion: Self-compassion is crucial in the face of setbacks and failures. Treat yourself
with kindness and understanding, acknowledging that eve-

ryone faces challenges and setbacks along their path. Avoid self-blame and negative self-talk. Instead, offer yourself support, encouragement, and forgiveness. By practicing self-compassion, you can bounce back with renewed confidence and motivation.

Analyze and Learn: When faced with a setback or failure, take the time to analyze what went wrong and learn from the experience. Reflect on the factors that contributed to the setback, identify areas for improvement, and develop a plan to address them. Use setbacks as opportunities for self reflection and personal growth. Adjust your strategies and actions based on the insights gained, setting yourself up for future success.

Seek Support: During challenging times, it is important to seek support from trusted friends, mentors, or a support network. Share your experience and seek guidance and perspective from those who can offer valuable insights. Surround yourself with individuals who believe in your potential and can provide encouragement and constructive feedback. Their support can help you regain confidence and provide a fresh perspective on your journey.

Set Realistic Expectations: When faced with setbacks or failures, re-evaluate your expectations and goals. Set realistic and attainable objectives that consider the lessons learned from the setback. Adjusting your expectations helps manage disappointment and enables you to focus on achievable milestones. Celebrate small victories along the way, building momentum and boosting your confidence.

Maintain a Positive Mindset: Maintaining a positive mindset is crucial when bouncing back from setbacks and failures. Focus on the progress you have made, the lessons learned, and the opportunities that lie ahead. Surround yourself with positivity, gratitude, and affirmations. By nurturing a positive mindset, you can overcome self-doubt and regain the motivation needed to move forward.

Take Action and Persist: The most important strategy for bouncing back is to take action and persist in the face of setbacks and failures. Use the lessons learned to adjust your approach, develop resilience, and maintain your determination. Remember that setbacks and failures are temporary obstacles on your journey. By taking consistent action, you move closer to your goals, armed with newfound wisdom and strength.

Bouncing back from setbacks and failures is an integral part of the journey to success and fulfillment. By embracing a growth mindset, practicing self-compassion, analyzing and learning from setbacks, seeking support, setting realistic expectations, maintaining a positive mindset, and taking persistent action, you can effectively navigate setbacks and failures. Remember, setbacks are not indicative of your worth or potential. They are stepping stones towards growth and achievement. Embrace the power of resilience and use setbacks as opportunities to ignite your journey to success and fulfillment.

CHAPTER 5: CONQUERING FEAR AND DOUBT

In Chapter 5, we explore extensively into the profound impact of fear and self-doubt on our journey to success and fulfillment. Fear and doubt can paralyze our progress, hinder our potential, and prevent us from taking that crucial first step towards our dreams. In this chapter, we explore strategies and insights that will enable us to conquer fear and doubt, empowering us to move forward with confidence, courage, and unwavering belief in our abilities.

Fear and doubt are natural emotions that arise when we step outside our comfort zones or face uncertainty. They can manifest as a fear of failure, fear of judgment, fear of the unknown, or a lack of confidence in our capabilities. Understanding the origins and triggers of fear and doubt is essential in order to address and overcome them effectively. By acknowledging and dissecting these emotions, we gain insights into the underlying beliefs and thought patterns that contribute to our fears and doubts.

Fear and doubt often stem from limiting beliefs we hold about ourselves and our potential. These beliefs can be deeply ingrained and rooted in past experiences or external influences. In this chapter, we explore techniques to challenge and reframe these limiting beliefs. By recognizing that our beliefs are not fixed or absolute, we can replace self-limiting thoughts with empowering beliefs that support our growth, progress, and pursuit of our dreams.

Self-confidence is the antidote to fear and doubt. In this chapter, we will immerse ourselves into strategies for cultivating and strengthening our self-confidence. From practicing self-affirmations and positive self-talk to celebrating our achievements and embracing a growth mindset, we explore various techniques that boost our self-confidence. By cultivating a strong belief in ourselves and our abilities, we become better equipped to face challenges and overcome self-doubt.

Fear and doubt often intensify when we experience failure. However, failure is an inevitable part of any journey towards success. In this chapter, we explore the importance of developing resilience in the face of failure. We delve into techniques for reframing failure as a learning opportunity, embracing a growth mindset, and persisting in the face of setbacks. By viewing failure as a stepping stone to growth and reframing our perspectives, we can bounce back stronger and more determined than ever before.

In conquering fear and doubt, mindset shifts and visualization techniques play a powerful role. We will explore the impact of positive mindset shifts and visualization exercises on overcoming fear and doubt.

By shifting our focus from potential obstacles to opportunities, visualizing success, and engaging in positive self-talk, we can rewire our minds to embrace courage and confidence. These techniques help us reprogram our subconscious beliefs and align our thoughts with our aspirations.

Chapter 5 emphasizes the importance of conquering fear and doubt on our journey to success and fulfillment.

By understanding the origins of fear and doubt, challenging limiting beliefs, cultivating self-confidence, developing resilience in the face of failure, and employing mindset shifts and visualization techniques, we can overcome the barriers that hold us back. With the tools and strategies provided in this chapter, we can conquer fear and doubt, unlocking our true potential and propelling ourselves forward on the path to success and fulfillment.

IDENTIFYING AND OVERCOMING LIMITING BELIEFS

The first step in overcoming limiting beliefs is to recognize their presence in our lives. Limiting beliefs can be subtle and deeply rooted, making them challenging to identify. Through self-reflection and introspection, we uncover the underlying beliefs that hinder our progress and hold us back from pursuing our dreams. By becoming aware of these limiting beliefs, we gain the power to challenge and transform them.

Once we have identified our limiting beliefs, it is crucial to question their validity. Many limiting beliefs are based on assumptions, generalizations, or outdated information. In this chapter, we explore strategies to challenge the accuracy and truthfulness of these beliefs. We examine the evidence that supports or refutes our beliefs, seeking alternative perspectives and considering the possibilities beyond our self-imposed limitations.

To overcome limiting beliefs, we must reframe and shift our perspectives. In this chapter, we delve into techniques that help us reinterpret our experiences, thoughts, and self-perceptions. We explore the power of positive affirmations, reframing negative self-talk, and consciously choosing empowering beliefs. By reframing our perspectives, we transform our limiting beliefs into empowering ones that support our growth, success, and fulfillment.

Replacing limiting beliefs with empowering beliefs is a vital step in the process of personal transformation. In this chapter, we delve into practical strategies to develop and reinforce empowering beliefs. We explore the use of visualization exercises, positive self-talk, and affirmations to solidify new beliefs that align with our aspirations. By consistently reinforcing these empowering beliefs, we reshape our mindset and open ourselves to new opportunities and possibilities.

Overcoming limiting beliefs can be a challenging journey. It is essential to seek support and accountability from trusted individuals who believe in our potential. In this chapter, we explore the importance of surrounding ourselves with a supportive network, such as mentors, coaches, or like-minded individuals. They can provide guidance, encouragement, and a fresh perspective to challenge our limiting beliefs. With their support, we gain the strength and motivation to persist in our journey towards personal growth and achievement.

The process of identifying and overcoming limiting beliefs is an ongoing one. We emphasize the importance of continual growth and self-reflection. We explore practices such as journaling, mindfulness, and regular self-assessment to maintain awareness of our beliefs and ensure that we remain on the path of personal growth and empowerment. By continuously challenging and overcoming limiting beliefs, we create a foundation for lifelong learning, resilience, and success.

Identifying and overcoming limiting beliefs is a transformative process that liberates us from self-imposed barriers.

By recognizing and challenging the validity of our limiting beliefs, reframing our perspectives, and replacing them with empowering beliefs, we unlock our true potential and open ourselves to new possibilities. With the support of a nurturing network and a commitment to continual growth and self-reflection, we can break free from the constraints of limiting beliefs and create a life of fulfillment, success, and personal empowerment.

HARNESSING THE POWER OF POSITIVE THINKING

We dive into the profound impact of positive thinking and how it intertwines with taking the first steps towards our dreams. We explore the transformative potential of cultivating a positive mindset and embracing the power of positive thinking, understanding how it sets the stage for success and fulfillment.

Positive thinking serves as a catalyst for taking the first steps on our journey. When we approach our goals and dreams with an optimistic outlook, we create a fertile ground for growth, resilience, and creativity. Positive thinking fuels our motivation, propelling us forward despite challenges and setbacks. It enables us to see opportunities where others see obstacles, empowering us to take those crucial first steps towards our aspirations.

By harnessing the power of positive thinking, we transform our perception of taking the first steps. Instead of viewing them as daunting or intimidating, we see them as exciting opportunities for growth and progress. Positive thinking helps us develop the courage to step outside our comfort zones, embrace uncertainty, and believe in our ability to overcome any obstacles that may arise along the way.

When we cultivate a positive mindset, we shift our focus from limitations to possibilities. We become more open to learning, adapting, and embracing change. Taking the first steps becomes a natural extension of our positive thinking, as we understand that each step we take brings us closer to our desired outcomes and ultimately contributes to our overall success and fulfillment.

Positive thinking also fosters resilience, which is essential for navigating the challenges that inevitably arise on our journey. When we encounter setbacks or face moments of doubt, a positive mindset helps us bounce back with determination and unwavering belief in ourselves. It enables us to reframe failures as learning experiences and motivates us to keep moving forward.

Moreover, positive thinking creates a ripple effect in our lives. As we take those first steps towards our dreams, our positive energy and optimism influence those around us. We become a source of inspiration and encouragement, inspiring others to embark on their own journeys of growth and self-discovery.

In conclusion, harnessing the power of positive thinking is not only crucial for igniting our journey to success and fulfillment but also for embracing the importance of taking the first steps. Positive thinking transforms our perspective, fuels our motivation, and enhances our resilience. It empowers us to overcome fear and self-doubt, replacing them with confidence and belief in our abilities. By embracing positive thinking and taking those initial steps, we set in motion a remarkable journey towards the realization of our dreams, experiencing the true power of a first step on the path to success and fulfillment.

Let us take a look into the powerful techniques for managing fear and self-doubt that can propel us forward on our path to success. We will explore the transformative potential of these techniques and how they relate to taking those crucial first steps towards our dreams.

Fear and self-doubt often act as barriers that hold us back from pursuing our goals and aspirations. They create a sense of uncertainty and undermine our confidence, making it difficult to take that initial leap of faith. However, when we learn to manage and overcome these challenges, we open the door to a world of possibilities and ignite our journey to success and fulfillment.

One of the key techniques we explore is the practice of self-awareness. By cultivating an understanding of our fears and self-doubts, we gain insights into their origins and patterns. We learn to recognize the negative thoughts and beliefs that contribute to our insecurities. Through this awareness, we can challenge and reframe these limiting beliefs, replacing them with empowering ones that fuel our confidence and propel us forward.

Another powerful technique is the cultivation of courage. Taking the first steps requires courage, as it involves stepping out of our comfort zones and venturing into the unknown. We explore strategies for building courage, such as setting small achievable goals, celebrating small victories, and gradually expanding our comfort zones. By embracing courage, we shift our mindset from fear to bravery, empowering ourselves to take those vital first steps towards our dreams.

Additionally, we analyze the practice of visualization and positive affirmation. These techniques involve creating a clear mental image of our desired outcomes and affirming positive beliefs about ourselves and our capabilities. Through visualization, we align our thoughts and emotions with our goals, boosting our confidence and motivation. Positive affirmations help rewire our subconscious mind, replacing self-doubt with self-belief. By consistently practicing visualization and positive affirmations, we strengthen our mental resilience and set the stage for success.

Furthermore, we explore the significance of taking calculated risks. It's essential to recognize that growth and success often require us to step outside our comfort zones and embrace uncertainty. We learn how to assess risks, evaluate potential rewards, and make informed decisions. By embracing a mindset of calculated risk-taking, we build resilience and confidence, allowing us to overcome fear and self-doubt and seize opportunities that align with our goals.

Taking the first steps ignites our journey to success and fulfillment because it represents a commitment to ourselves and our dreams. It signifies our willingness to confront our fears and self-doubts head-on, stepping into the realm of possibility and growth. By managing fear and self-doubt through these techniques, we create a strong foundation for progress and achievement. Each step we take not only brings us closer to our goals but also strengthens our belief in ourselves and our ability to overcome obstacles. In conclusion, techniques for managing fear and self-doubt are crucial for igniting our journey to success and fulfillment.

By cultivating self-awareness, courage, visualization, positive affirmation, and calculated risk-taking, we overcome the barriers that hold us back and propel ourselves forward. Taking the first steps becomes a transformative experience that fuels our confidence, expands our horizons, and sets the stage for a remarkable journey of growth, accomplishment, and personal fulfillment.

CHAPTER 6: EMBRACING FAILURE AS A STEPPING STONE

In chapter 6, we examine closely the transformative concept of embracing failure as a stepping stone on our path to success. We explore the profound impact of this mindset shift and how it relates to taking those crucial first steps towards our dreams.

Failure is often viewed as something to be feared and avoided. It carries a negative connotation and is often associated with disappointment and setbacks. However, when we learn to embrace failure as a valuable learning experience and a necessary part of the journey, we unlock the potential for growth, resilience, and ultimate success.

One of the key reasons why taking the first steps ignites our journey to success and fulfillment is because it exposes us to the possibility of failure. By venturing into uncharted territory and pursuing our dreams, we step out of our comfort zones and confront the inherent risks that come with it. This initial step represents our willingness to face uncertainty and overcome the fear of failure, which is a powerful catalyst for personal and professional growth.

When we embrace failure as a stepping stone, we shift our perspective from viewing it as a setback to seeing it as a valuable teacher. Each failure becomes an opportunity to learn, reflect, and improve. We gain insights into our strengths, weaknesses, and areas for development. By embracing failure, we become resilient individuals who are better equipped to navigate challenges, adapt to change, and persevere in the face of adversity.

Furthermore, embracing failure allows us to develop a growth mindset. Rather than seeing failure as a reflection of our worth or abilities, we recognize that it is a natural part of the learning process. Failure becomes a stepping stone towards success, as it provides valuable feedback and helps us refine our strategies and approaches. By embracing failure and learning from it, we continuously evolve and improve, increasing our chances of achieving our goals and finding fulfillment in our endeavors.

Taking the first steps and embracing failure go hand in hand because they require courage, resilience, and a belief in our own potential. By acknowledging that failure is not a permanent state but a temporary setback, we free ourselves from the fear of making mistakes. This new-found freedom empowers us to take bolder risks, explore new opportunities, and push beyond our perceived limitations.

In conclusion, embracing failure as a stepping stone is essential for igniting our journey to success and fulfillment.

By viewing failure as a valuable learning experience, we transform setbacks into opportunities for growth and improvement.

Taking the first steps becomes a transformative act of courage and resilience, as it signifies our willingness to embrace both success and failure as integral parts of our journey. By adopting this mindset, we pave the way for continuous learning, personal growth, and ultimately, the achievement of our goals and the fulfillment of our dreams.

REDEFINING FAILURE AND EMBRACING IT AS A LEARNING OPPORTUNITY

Failure is often seen as a negative outcome, synonymous with defeat and disappointment. However, when we redefine failure and view it as a stepping stone rather than a roadblock, we unlock a world of possibilities for growth, resilience, and ultimate success.

One of the reasons why taking the first steps ignites our journey to success and fulfillment is because it exposes us to the possibility of failure. By stepping out of our comfort zones and pursuing our dreams, we venture into uncharted territory where failure may occur. This initial step signifies our willingness to embrace the unknown and take calculated risks, which is a powerful catalyst for personal and professional growth.

By redefining failure, we shift our perspective from seeing it as an end point to viewing it as a valuable learning experience. Failure becomes an opportunity for reflection, introspection, and improvement. Each setback becomes a chance to assess our strategies, identify areas for development, and gain valuable insights that can guide us on our path to success.

When we embrace failure as a learning opportunity, we develop a growth mindset. Instead of allowing failure to discourage or define us, we recognize that it is an integral part of the journey towards success. We understand that failure is not a reflection of our worth or capabilities but rather a stepping stone towards improvement and eventual achievement. By embracing failure, we foster resilience, adaptability, and perseverance in the face of challenges.

Moreover, redefining failure and embracing it as a learning opportunity empowers us to overcome the fear of failure. Fear often holds us back from taking those crucial first steps towards our dreams. However, when we redefine failure as a natural part of the learning process, we liberate ourselves from the paralyzing grip of fear. This newfound freedom allows us to take bolder risks, explore new possibilities, and fully engage in our journey towards success and fulfillment.

By taking the first steps and embracing failure as a learning opportunity, we embark on a transformative journey of self-discovery and growth. We recognize that failure is not an endpoint but a stepping stone towards success. Each failure becomes a valuable lesson, guiding us towards better strategies, deeper self-awareness, and ultimately, a clearer path to our goals.

Redefining failure and embracing it as a learning opportunity is vital for igniting our journey to success and fulfillment.

By shifting our perspective, we unlock the potential for growth, resilience, and personal development. Taking the first steps becomes an act of courage, as we acknowledge that failure is an inherent part of the journey towards success. By embracing failure and embracing the lessons it offers, we pave the way for continuous improvement, increased resilience, and the realization of our dreams.

A growth mindset entails the conviction that our abilities and intelligence can be cultivated through dedication, exertion, and a receptive attitude towards acquiring knowledge. It is about embracing challenges, persisting in the face of setbacks, and seeing failures as opportunities for growth. By cultivating a growth mindset, we ignite our journey to success and fulfillment in numerous ways.

One of the reasons why taking the first steps ignites our journey to success and fulfillment is because it requires a growth mindset. Stepping out of our comfort zones and pursuing our dreams can be intimidating and challenging. However, with a growth mindset, we approach these endeavors as opportunities for personal growth and development. We view challenges as stepping stones, knowing that our abilities can be cultivated and improved over time through dedication and effort.

Cultivating a growth mindset enables us to embrace the learning process. We understand that setbacks and failures are not indications of our limitations but rather part of the journey towards mastery. With this mindset, we seek feedback, learn from our mistakes, and continuously strive to improve. Taking the first steps becomes an exciting and fulfilling endeavor, as we see each step as an opportunity to learn, grow, and become better versions of ourselves.

Additionally, a growth mindset fuels resilience and perseverance. When faced with obstacles or setbacks, we see them as temporary hurdles that can be overcome through effort and learning. Rather than giving up in the face of challenges, we persist, adapt, and find alternative strategies to move forward. By cultivating a growth mindset, we develop the resilience necessary to navigate the ups and downs of our journey, staying focused on our goals and moving closer to success.

Furthermore, a growth mindset nurtures a sense of possibility and optimism. Instead of being limited by self-imposed beliefs, we believe in our potential to learn, grow, and achieve our dreams. We recognize that our abilities are not fixed but can be expanded with effort and practice. Taking the first steps becomes an empowering act, as we trust in our ability to develop the skills and knowledge needed to succeed.

Cultivating a growth mindset is crucial for igniting our journey to success and fulfillment. By embracing challenges, persisting in the face of setbacks, and seeing failures as opportunities for growth, we open ourselves up to incredible possibilities. Taking the first steps becomes a transformative experience, as we approach our goals with a mindset of continuous learning, resilience, and optimism. With a growth mindset, we unlock our potential, overcome limitations, and embark on a journey of personal and professional growth that leads us to the fulfillment of our dreams.

We investigate in detail the transformative concept of leveraging failures to propel our progress and its profound impact on our path to success. We delve into the importance of reframing failures and using them as stepping stones towards achieving our dreams. By understanding how failures can ignite our journey, we unlock the potential for growth, resilience, and ultimate fulfillment.

One of the key reasons why taking the first steps ignites our journey to success and fulfillment is because it exposes us to the possibility of failure. Stepping outside our comfort zones and pursuing our dreams means venturing into the unknown, where obstacles and setbacks are inevitable. However, it is through these failures that we gain valuable insights and experiences that propel us forward. Taking that initial step signifies our readiness to embrace the challenges and uncertainties that may arise, knowing that each failure can serve as a catalyst for progress. By leveraging failures, we shift our perspective from seeing them as dead ends to viewing them as opportunities for growth and learning. Instead of being discouraged or disheartened by failures, we recognize them as valuable lessons. Each setback becomes a chance to assess our strategies, re-evaluate our approach, and make necessary adjustments to move closer to success. Failures provide us with valuable feedback, highlighting areas where we can improve and guiding us towards more effective paths.

Moreover, failures foster resilience and perseverance. When we encounter obstacles or experience setbacks, it is easy to become disheartened and lose motivation. However, by leveraging failures, we develop resilience and the ability to bounce back stronger. We learn to adapt, pivot, and find alternative routes towards our goals. Each failure becomes an opportunity to develop the mental strength needed to overcome challenges and stay committed to our journey.

Furthermore, leveraging failures ignites innovation and creativity. When our initial approaches don't yield the desired results, failures force us to think outside the box and explore alternative solutions. We become open to new ideas, approaches, and perspectives. Taking the first steps becomes an opportunity to tap into our creative potential, as we embrace failures as opportunities for innovation and growth.

By leveraging failures, we also cultivate a growth mindset. We understand that failures are not indicators of our worth or potential, but rather temporary setbacks on the path to success. We shift from a fixed mindset, which views failures as personal shortcomings, to a growth mindset, which sees failures as stepping stones towards improvement. This mindset shift empowers us to persevere, embrace challenges, and continue learning and growing.

Leveraging failures to propel our progress is a vital aspect of igniting our journey to success and fulfillment.

By reframing failures as valuable learning experiences, we transform setbacks into stepping stones. Taking the first steps becomes an act of courage and resilience, as we understand that failures are an integral part of the growth process. By leveraging failures, we gain insights, develop resilience, foster innovation, and cultivate a growth mindset. We embrace failures as opportunities for growth and propel ourselves forward on the path to success and ultimate fulfillment.

PART THREE: TAKING AC-
TION

CHAPTER 7: PLANNING YOUR JOURNEY

Chapter 7 focuses on the crucial step of planning your journey towards success. We explore the significance of effective planning and how it plays a pivotal role in igniting your path towards achieving your goals and finding fulfillment.

Taking the first steps ignites your journey to success and fulfillment because it marks the beginning of your intentional and purposeful planning process. By initiating action and embarking on your journey, you shift from merely dreaming or wishing for success to actively strategizing and creating a roadmap to reach your desired destination.

Planning plays a fundamental role in guiding your actions and keeping you focused on your goals. It helps you clarify your vision, define your objectives, and outline the necessary steps to move forward. Through planning, you gain a clear understanding of what you want to achieve and the specific actions required to get there. Taking the first steps becomes an empowering act, as it signifies your commitment to turning your aspirations into tangible reality.

Moreover, planning provides structure and organization to your journey. It helps you break down your goals into smaller, manageable tasks, making them less daunting and more achievable. By setting milestones and deadlines, you create a sense of purpose and urgency, propelling you forward with a sense of direction and motivation.

Taking the first steps becomes a catalyst for progress, as it sets the stage for implementing your well-thought-out plan.

Additionally, planning allows for flexibility and adaptability. While it's important to have a roadmap, it's equally crucial to embrace the fact that unforeseen circumstances and opportunities may arise along the way. Effective planning takes into account potential obstacles, alternative routes, and contingency plans. By anticipating and preparing for potential challenges, you equip yourself with the necessary tools and mindset to navigate the journey with resilience and adaptability. Taking the first steps becomes an act of preparedness, as you are ready to face the uncertainties and adapt your plans as needed.

Furthermore, planning instills a sense of accountability and commitment. When you have a well-defined plan in place, you create a sense of responsibility to follow through on your intentions. It becomes easier to track your progress, evaluate your actions, and make necessary adjustments. By committing to your plan and holding yourself accountable, you reinforce your determination and motivation to continue taking steps forward. Taking the first steps becomes an act of personal commitment, as you honor the plan you have set for yourself and stay true to your aspirations. Chapter 7 emphasizes the importance of planning your journey towards success and fulfillment. By taking the first steps and initiating the planning process, you ignite your path towards achieving your goals. Effective planning provides you with clarity, structure, and accountability, ensuring that your actions are aligned with your aspirations.

It allows for flexibility and adaptability, empowering you to navigate challenges and embrace opportunities along the way. By planning your journey, you set the stage for a purposeful and intentional pursuit of success and fulfillment.

We will explore the crucial concept of developing a roadmap to success and its profound impact on igniting your path towards achieving your goals and finding fulfillment.

Developing a roadmap to success is essential because it provides a clear and strategic plan that guides your actions and decisions. It serves as a blueprint that outlines the necessary steps, milestones, and resources needed to progress towards your desired outcomes. Taking the first steps becomes the catalyst for igniting your journey, as it signifies your commitment to creating a roadmap that will lead you to success and fulfillment.

One of the key reasons why developing a roadmap is vital is because it enhances your focus and clarity. When you have a well-defined plan in place, you gain a sense of direction and purpose. You understand where you are currently and where you want to go. Each step you take becomes purposeful and aligned with your overarching goals. By developing a roadmap, you eliminate distractions and prioritize the actions that will bring you closer to your desired destination.

Moreover, a roadmap provides a framework for setting achievable goals and milestones. It allows you to break down your long-term objectives into smaller, manageable tasks. By setting specific and measurable milestones, you create a sense of progress and accomplishment along the way. Celebrating these milestones boosts your motivation and fuels your drive to keep moving forward. Taking the first steps becomes the initial leap towards achieving these milestones and inching closer to your ultimate success.

Additionally, a roadmap helps you anticipate and navigate potential obstacles and challenges. It prompts you to identify potential roadblocks that may arise and develop contingency plans to overcome them. By considering various scenarios and having backup strategies, you equip yourself with the resilience and adaptability needed to navigate setbacks. Taking the first steps becomes an act of preparedness, as you have thoughtfully planned for potential hurdles and are ready to face them head-on. Furthermore, a roadmap encourages accountability and progress tracking. When you have a detailed plan, you can monitor your progress and evaluate your actions effectively. Regularly assessing your advancement allows you to make necessary adjustments and stay on course. By holding yourself accountable to the roadmap, you maintain focus and motivation to continue taking consistent steps towards success. Taking the first steps becomes an act of personal responsibility, as you honor the commitment to follow the roadmap you have laid out for yourself.

In conclusion, developing a roadmap to success is an integral part of igniting your journey towards achievement and fulfillment.

By taking the first steps and initiating the development of a strategic plan, you set the stage for intentional and purposeful progress.

A roadmap enhances your focus, sets achievable goals, prepares you for challenges, and fosters accountability. It empowers you to navigate your journey with clarity, resilience, and progress.

By developing a roadmap, you ignite the path to success and fulfillment, transforming your aspirations into tangible realities.

Creating an action plan is essential because it transforms your aspirations into concrete steps and actionable tasks. It takes your vision and breaks it down into manageable actions that move you closer to your desired outcomes. Taking the first steps becomes the catalyst for igniting your journey, as it signifies your commitment to creating an action plan that will propel you towards success and fulfillment.

One of the key reasons why creating an action plan is crucial is because it provides clarity and structure. When you have a well-defined plan in place, you gain a clear understanding of the specific actions required to achieve your goals. It outlines the steps you need to take, the resources you need to gather, and the timelines you need to follow. By creating an action plan, you eliminate confusion and ensure that each step you take aligns with your ultimate objectives.

Moreover, an action plan brings focus and prioritization to your journey. It helps you identify the most critical tasks and allocate your time, energy, and resources accordingly. By setting priorities and organizing your actions, you optimize your productivity and maximize your chances of success. Taking the first steps becomes the initiation of this focused approach, as you start implementing the action plan and directing your efforts towards the key tasks that will lead you to achievement and fulfillment.

Additionally, an action plan facilitates progress tracking and accountability. It allows you to monitor your advancement, assess your performance, and make necessary
adjustments along the way. By breaking down your goals
into smaller milestones and tasks, you create measurable
checkpoints that enable you to gauge your progress. Regularly reviewing your action plan helps you stay on track
and ensures that you are consistently moving forward.
Taking the first steps becomes an act of accountability, as
you honor the commitment to follow through on the tasks
outlined in your action plan.

Furthermore, an action plan enhances motivation and
momentum. When you have a detailed plan in place, you
can celebrate small victories and witness the progress you
are making. Each completed task becomes a source of motivation that propels you forward. The sense of accomplishment and forward momentum generated by taking the
first steps fuels your drive to continue taking consistent
action. It reinforces your belief in your ability to achieve
your goals and strengthens your determination to see your
journey through.

Creating an action plan is a vital component of igniting your path to achievement and fulfillment. By taking
the first steps and developing an actionable plan, you set
the stage for purposeful and intentional progress. An action plan provides clarity, focus, progress tracking, and
accountability. It ensures that your efforts are aligned with
your goals and optimizes your chances of success. By cre-

ating an action plan, you ignite the path towards achievement and fulfillment, transforming your dreams into tangible outcomes.

Breaking down goals into manageable steps is essential because it allows you to turn seemingly daunting objectives into actionable tasks. It takes big, overarching goals and breaks them down into smaller, more attainable milestones that are easier to tackle. Taking the first steps becomes the catalyst for igniting progress, as it signifies your commitment to breaking down your goals and taking the initial strides towards their accomplishment.

One of the key reasons why breaking down goals is crucial is because it provides clarity and focus. When you break down a goal into smaller steps, you gain a clear understanding of the specific actions required to achieve it. Each step becomes a tangible and manageable task that you can tackle with confidence. By breaking down goals, you eliminate overwhelm and ensure that you have a clear roadmap for progressing towards your desired outcomes.

Moreover, breaking down goals into manageable steps enhances motivation and momentum. When you set smaller milestones, you create opportunities for celebrating achievements along the way. Each completed step becomes a mini-victory that fuels your motivation to keep moving forward. The sense of accomplishment generated by taking the first steps propels you to continue taking action and builds positive momentum towards the attainment of your larger goals. Breaking down goals becomes an empowering process, as it helps you maintain a sense of progress and fuels your enthusiasm on the journey.

Additionally, breaking down goals facilitates better planning and resource allocation. When you have smaller steps, it becomes easier to allocate time, energy, and resources to each task. You can prioritize your efforts and determine the most efficient way to approach each step. By breaking down goals, you optimize your productivity and ensure that you are utilizing your resources effectively. Taking the first steps becomes the initiation of this strategic approach, as you begin executing the smaller tasks that collectively lead to the realization of your larger goals.

Furthermore, breaking down goals into manageable steps promotes resilience and adaptability. It allows you to adjust your approach as needed and pivot if circumstances change. By breaking goals into smaller components, you create flexibility in your journey. If you encounter obstacles or face unexpected challenges, you can reassess and modify your plan while maintaining progress. Breaking down goals becomes an act of preparedness, as you are ready to adapt and navigate the twists and turns that may arise along the way.

By taking the first steps and breaking down your goals, you set the stage for purposeful and achievable progress. Breaking down goals provides clarity, enhances motivation, enables better planning, and fosters resilience. It ensures that your efforts are focused, actionable, and adaptable. By breaking down goals, you ignite the path towards success and fulfillment, transforming your aspirations into tangible milestones one step at a time.

CHAPTER 8: TAKING THE FIRST STEP

We reach a pivotal chapter that explores the significance of taking the first step on your path towards transformation and personal growth.

Chapter 8 investigates the profound impact of initiating action and overcoming inertia. It highlights the importance of embracing the moment when you decide to step out of your comfort zone and embark on your journey to success and fulfillment. Taking the first step becomes the catalyst for igniting the spark of transformation within you, propelling you forward on a transformative and empowering trajectory.

This chapter emphasizes that taking the first step is

more than just a physical act—it is a powerful declaration of intent. It is the moment when you commit to your dreams, aspirations, and goals. By taking that initial leap, you demonstrate your belief in yourself and your willingness to embrace change. It is a bold and courageous act that sets in motion a series of events, opening doors to new possibilities and opportunities.

Taking the first step signifies your readiness to face challenges, overcome obstacles, and embrace growth. It is an act of courage, as it requires venturing into the unknown and embracing uncertainty. By stepping forward, you signal your determination to push past fear, self-doubt, and limitations. It is a transformative moment where you acknowledge that success and fulfillment lie beyond your comfort zone, and you are willing to embrace discomfort for the sake of personal growth

Furthermore, taking the first step generates momentum and builds positive energy. Once you break through the inertia and initiate action, you create a domino effect that propels you forward. Each subsequent step becomes easier as you build confidence and gather momentum. Taking the first step ignites a fire within you, fuelling your motivation, enthusiasm, and drive to continue progressing towards your goals.

We will also explore the power of resilience in the face of setbacks and obstacles. It reminds you that setbacks are not failures but valuable learning opportunities. By taking the first step, you develop the resilience needed to overcome challenges. You learn to adapt, pivot, and persevere, using each setback as a stepping stone towards growth and success. Taking the first step enables you to cultivate a mindset of resilience and embrace the journey as a continuous process of learning, growth, and self-discovery.

Within this section we explore some essential strategies that can help you overcome inertia and take action towards your dreams and goals. We will emphasize the importance of breaking free from the grip of stagnation and embracing a proactive mindset that propels you forward.

Overcoming inertia requires a conscious effort to disrupt the status quo and challenge the comfort of familiarity. It is about recognizing the patterns of complacency that can hold you back and actively seeking ways to overcome them. By implementing strategies tailored to overcome inertia, you can ignite the fire within and set your journey in motion.

One powerful strategy is to cultivate a compelling vision. Visualize the future you desire, paint a vivid picture of your aspirations, and connect emotionally with the possibilities that lie ahead. By anchoring yourself to a captivating vision, you create a sense of urgency and motivation that propels you past inertia. Your vision becomes the fuel that ignites the fire within, compelling you to take the necessary steps to turn your dreams into reality.

Another strategy is to set clear goals and establish actionable plans. Break down your objectives into specific, measurable, attainable, relevant, and time-bound (SMART) goals. By setting clear targets, you create a roadmap that guides your actions and eliminates ambiguity. Each step taken becomes a deliberate move towards progress, instilling a sense of purpose and direction.

Moreover, creating accountability systems can be instrumental in overcoming inertia. Share your goals and intentions with a trusted friend, mentor, or coach who can hold you accountable. Regular check-ins and progress reviews help maintain focus and keep you on track. Accountability provides the necessary external push and support that can break through the inertia and compel you to take action.

Additionally, adopting a growth mindset is key to overcoming inertia. Embrace a belief that challenges and setbacks are opportunities for growth and learning. Develop resilience and cultivate a positive attitude towards failure, viewing it as a stepping stone on your journey. By reframing obstacles as valuable learning experiences, you can transform inertia into a springboard for personal and professional development.

Furthermore, taking small, consistent steps is crucial in overcoming inertia. Break down tasks into manageable chunks, and commit to taking regular action. Even the tiniest step forward is a step away from inertia and towards progress. By establishing a habit of consistent effort, you build momentum and create a positive feedback loop that fuels further action.

Lastly, surround yourself with a supportive environment. Seek out individuals who inspire and motivate you. Engage in communities, workshops, or mentorship programs that provide encouragement and accountability. Surrounding yourself with like-minded individuals who share your aspirations can be a powerful catalyst for taking action and overcoming inertia

In conclusion, strategies to overcome inertia and take action are essential components of igniting the fire within and embarking on your journey to success and fulfillment. By cultivating a compelling vision, setting clear goals, establishing accountability, adopting a growth mindset, taking small steps, and surrounding yourself with a supportive environment, you can break free from inertia and initiate the transformative power of the first step. These strategies empower you to overcome obstacles, stay motivated, and create positive momentum on your path to achieving your dreams and aspirations.

Let us thoroughly examine a crucial topic that often hinders progress and growth—analysis paralysis. We will focus on understanding the nature of analysis paralysis and provide strategies to overcome it, empowering you to take decisive action and move forward on your journey.

Analysis paralysis refers to the state of being overwhelmed by the abundance of information, options, and possibilities, leading to indecision and a lack of action. It is a mental and emotional trap that can hinder progress and keep you stuck in a perpetual cycle of overthinking and overanalyzing.

To overcome analysis paralysis, it is crucial to recognize the underlying causes and address them head-on. One common cause is the fear of making mistakes or choosing the wrong path. The chapter encourages you to embrace a mindset that views mistakes as valuable learning opportunities and recognizes that taking action is better than remaining stagnant. By reframing mistakes as stepping stones to growth, you can shift your perspective and break free from the paralyzing fear of making decisions.

Another strategy is to focus on gathering relevant information rather than seeking perfection. Recognize that complete certainty is rarely attainable, and waiting for perfect conditions may lead to missed opportunities. Instead, aim to gather sufficient information to make an informed decision and trust your judgment. Remember that progress and growth often come from taking calculated risks and stepping outside your comfort zone.

Setting deadlines and creating a sense of urgency is another effective way to overcome analysis paralysis. By establishing time constraints, you create a sense of accountability and compel yourself to make decisions within a specified timeframe. This approach encourages action and prevents unnecessary delays caused by excessive contemplation.

Breaking down complex tasks or decisions into smaller, manageable steps can also help overcome analysis paralysis. By dissecting the process, you make it less overwhelming and easier to tackle. This approach allows you to focus on one step at a time, making progress while reducing the mental burden of considering the entire scope of the task.

Moreover, trusting your intuition and gut instincts can be invaluable in overcoming analysis paralysis. Sometimes, overthinking can cloud your judgment and lead to indecision. By tapping into your inner wisdom and listening to your intuition, you can gain clarity and make decisions with greater confidence. Trusting yourself and your instincts empowers you to move forward with conviction.

Lastly, cultivating a mindset of flexibility and adaptability is crucial in overcoming analysis paralysis. Recognize that decisions are not set in stone and can be adjusted along the way. Embrace the idea of learning and course correction, allowing yourself to iterate and refine your approach as you gain more insights and experience.

By implementing these strategies to overcome analysis paralysis, you unleash the power of action and decision-making. You break free from the paralysis of overthinking and step into the realm of progress and growth. Taking the first step becomes easier as you embrace a mindset that values action, acknowledges the imperfections of decision-making, and recognizes that forward momentum is more important than getting everything perfect. Through these strategies, you unlock the potential to ignite your journey to success and fulfillment.

Decisive action is the act of making choices and taking deliberate steps towards your goals and aspirations. It involves overcoming hesitations, doubts, and uncertainties and instead, boldly moving forward with purpose and determination. By celebrating decisive action, you acknowledge the importance of seizing opportunities and capitalizing on the power of momentum.

One of the key reasons why decisive action is vital is that it propels you past the realm of contemplation and into the realm of tangible progress. Taking action is the catalyst that sets your journey in motion, creating a ripple effect of positive outcomes and opportunities. Each step taken builds upon the previous one, leading to a sense of accomplishment, growth, and fulfillment.

Decisive action also fosters a mindset of empowerment and self-belief. When you take the initiative to make decisions and act upon them, you demonstrate trust in your abilities and your capacity to create meaningful change. This mindset shift cultivates a sense of confidence and resilience, allowing you to navigate challenges and setbacks with a proactive mindset.

Furthermore, celebrating decisive action helps you develop a positive relationship with failure. Recognize that not every action will yield the desired results, but each action is an opportunity for learning and growth. By celebrating the courage and effort behind taking action, you reframe failure as a stepping stone towards improvement and success. This mindset shift allows you to embrace challenges as valuable lessons, leading to personal and professional development.

Celebrating decisive action also creates a sense of accountability and responsibility. By acknowledging the importance of taking ownership of your choices and actions, you become proactive in shaping your destiny. You understand that your success and fulfillment are within your control and that every decision you make plays a significant role in your journey.

Moreover, celebrating decisive action inspires and motivates others around you. Your actions serve as a source of inspiration, showing others what is possible when they step out of their comfort zones and embrace their dreams. By sharing your experiences and celebrating your achievements, you become a beacon of encouragement, sparking a ripple effect of positive action in your community.

Celebrating the power of decisive action is a testament to the transformative impact it has on your journey to success and fulfillment. By recognizing the significance of taking action, you embrace momentum, achievement, and personal growth. Through decisive action, you cultivate a mindset of empowerment, learn from failures, take ownership of your choices, and inspire those around you.

By celebrating decisive action, you unlock the true potential of your journey, propelling yourself towards a life filled with purpose, accomplishment, and joy.

CHAPTER 9: SUSTAINING MOMENTUM

Sustaining momentum is about cultivating habits, mindset, and strategies that enable you to continue making progress towards your goals. It involves avoiding complacency, staying motivated and overcoming obstacles that may arise along the way. This chapter provides valuable insights and practical techniques to help you stay on track and keep the fire of progress burning.

One of the fundamental aspects of sustaining momentum is establishing routines and rituals that support your goals. By creating consistent practices and structures in your daily life, you create a foundation for continued growth and progress. Whether it's dedicating specific times for focused work, incorporating self-care activities, or engaging in regular reflection and goal-setting, these routines provide a framework that helps you stay aligned with your aspirations.

Another crucial element in sustaining momentum is maintaining a growth mindset. Embracing a mindset of continuous learning, adaptation, and improvement allows you to navigate challenges and setbacks with resilience. It encourages you to view obstacles as opportunities for growth and fosters a sense of curiosity and open-mindedness. With a growth mindset, you remain flexible, embrace change, and constantly seek ways to expand your knowledge and skills.

Celebrating milestones and small victories along the way is crucial in sustaining momentum. Acknowledging and appreciating your progress reinforces a positive mind-set and fuels your motivation. Celebrations can take various forms, such as treating yourself, sharing achievements with loved ones, or reflecting on how far you've come. These moments of celebration serve as reminders of your growth and fuel the determination to continue moving forward.

Self-care and well-being are essential for sustaining momentum. Taking care of your physical, mental, and emotional health ensures that you have the energy and resilience to keep going. Prioritizing self-care activities, such as exercise, rest, mindfulness, and nurturing relation-ships, helps you maintain balance and replenish your energy reserves.

Finally, adaptability and course correction are key to sustaining momentum. As you progress on your journey, circumstances may change, and new opportunities may arise. Being open to adjusting your plans, embracing new strategies, and seizing unforeseen possibilities allows you to stay agile and adaptable. It ensures that you remain aligned with your aspirations and continue moving forward despite the ever-evolving nature of life.

Chapter 9 of "The Power of a First Step: Ignite Your Journey to Success and Fulfillment" emphasizes the significance of sustaining momentum in your pursuit of success and fulfillment. By establishing routines, cultivating a growth mindset, embracing accountability, celebrating achievements, prioritizing self-care, and embracing adaptability, you nurture the consistency and progress needed to sustain momentum. This chapter serves as a guide to help you navigate the challenges and maintain the positive trajectory of your journey, ensuring that you continue to thrive and make meaningful strides towards your goals.

CULTIVATING DISCIPLINE AND CONSIS-
TENCY

We investigate in details the crucial topic of cultivating discipline and consistency. Chapter 9 focuses on the importance of developing these qualities as essential components for achieving lasting success.

Discipline is the ability to consistently adhere to a set of actions, principles, or values that align with your goals. It is the commitment to follow through on your intentions, even when faced with challenges or distractions. Consistency, on the other hand, is the act of repeatedly taking the necessary steps towards your goals, day after day, without wavering.

Cultivating discipline and consistency is vital because they form the bedrock of sustainable progress. They provide the structure and foundation that keep you focused, motivated, and moving forward, even in the face of obstacles. Without discipline and consistency, it becomes challenging to stay on track and achieve your desired outcomes.

One of the key benefits of cultivating discipline and consistency is the development of positive habits. When you consistently engage in specific actions aligned with your goals, these actions become ingrained as habits. Over time, these habits become automatic and require less effort to maintain. By cultivating discipline and consistency, you pave the way for these positive habits to support your journey towards success and fulfillment.

Discipline and consistency also foster resilience and mental toughness. They enable you to persevere through difficult times and push past the moments of doubt, fatigue, or temptation. When faced with obstacles, disciplined individuals are more likely to stay committed, find alternative solutions, and maintain their focus on the long-term vision. Consistency reinforces the belief that progress is made through sustained effort and dedication.

Furthermore, cultivating discipline and consistency instills a sense of personal responsibility and accountability. When you commit to a course of action and consistently follow through, you take ownership of your journey. You recognize that your success is dependent on your actions and choices. This mindset empowers you to make proactive decisions, evaluate your progress, and make adjustments as needed.

Consistency also builds trust and credibility, both within yourself and with others. When you consistently deliver on your commitments, you demonstrate reliability and integrity. Others begin to trust in your abilities and rely on you to follow through. Self-trust is equally crucial, as it strengthens your belief in your own capabilities and fosters a positive self-image.

Cultivating discipline and consistency requires intentional effort and practice. It involves setting clear goals, establishing routines, managing your time effectively, and prioritizing tasks that align with your objectives. It may also involve creating systems of accountability, seeking support from mentors or coaches, and staying focused on the long-term rewards that come from consistent action.

By nurturing discipline and consistency, you develop positive habits, build resilience, take personal responsibility, and earn the trust of others. Through intentional effort and practice, you lay the foundation for sustained progress and propel yourself forward on the path to success and fulfillment.

Obstacles are a natural part of any endeavor, and they can take various forms such as setbacks, unexpected events, self-doubt, or external circumstances. Overcoming obstacles requires resilience, adaptability, and a commitment to staying focused on your goals. This chapter offers insights and strategies to help you navigate challenges effectively and maintain your focus amidst adversity.

One of the key aspects of overcoming obstacles is developing a growth mindset. A growth mindset enables you to perceive challenges as opportunities for learning and growth. Instead of viewing obstacles as roadblocks, you see them as stepping stones towards your desired outcomes. By embracing a growth mindset, you can cultivate the belief that with effort, perseverance, and learning from setbacks, you can overcome any obstacle that comes your way.

Staying focused is another crucial element in overcoming obstacles. It involves maintaining clarity about your goals, priorities, and the steps required to achieve them. When faced with challenges, staying focused allows you to channel your energy and resources towards finding solutions and making progress. It helps you avoid getting sidetracked by distractions or temporary setbacks, enabling you to stay committed to your long-term vision.

Resilience plays a significant role in overcoming obstacles and staying focused. Resilience is the ability to bounce back from setbacks, adapt to change, and maintain a positive mindset amidst adversity. It involves developing emotional strength, perseverance, and the willingness to learn from failures. With resilience, you can navigate obstacles with greater ease, maintain your focus, and keep moving forward despite the challenges that arise.

Effective problem-solving skills are essential for overcoming obstacles. When faced with a challenge, it is crucial to approach it with a proactive mindset. This involves analyzing the situation, identifying potential solutions, and taking decisive action. By developing effective problem-solving skills, you can tackle obstacles head-on and find innovative ways to overcome them.

Support systems and networks also play a vital role in overcoming obstacles. Surrounding yourself with a supportive community of like-minded individuals, mentors, or coaches can provide valuable guidance, encouragement, and perspective. These support systems can offer insights, share experiences, and provide the necessary motivation to help you stay focused and navigate challenges more effectively.

Furthermore, maintaining a positive and optimistic outlook can significantly impact your ability to overcome obstacles. By focusing on the possibilities, maintaining a positive attitude, and reframing challenges as opportunities for growth, you can stay motivated and resilient in the face of adversity. Cultivating a positive mindset helps you maintain your focus and allows you to approach obstacles with a solution-oriented mindset.

This book emphasizes the importance of overcoming obstacles and staying focused. By developing a growth mindset, staying focused on your goals, cultivating resilience, honing problem-solving skills, seeking support, and maintaining a positive outlook, you can navigate challenges effectively and stay on track towards achieving your aspirations. Through the strategies and insights provided in this chapter, you can overcome obstacles with determination and maintain the focus needed to continue your journey towards success and fulfillment.

Motivation is the internal force that propels you towards action and sustains your commitment to achieving your dreams. However, it's natural for motivation to fluctuate over time, especially when faced with challenges, setbacks, or the monotony of daily routines. Therefore, it is vital to employ strategies that can keep your motivation levels high and help you stay focused on your journey to success and fulfillment.

One effective strategy for maintaining motivation is to clarify and reconnect with your purpose. Take the time to reflect on why your goals matter to you and how they align with your values and aspirations. Understanding the deeper meaning behind your endeavors can reignite your passion and provide a powerful source of motivation. Regularly revisit your purpose and remind yourself of the impact your actions can have on your life and the lives of others.

Setting specific, meaningful, and achievable goals is another crucial strategy. Break down your larger goals into smaller milestones and celebrate each achievement along the way. This not only provides a sense of accomplishment but also fuels your motivation to progress further. By setting clear goals, you create a roadmap that keeps you focused and gives you a sense of direction throughout your journey.

Regularly visualizing your desired outcomes can also be a powerful motivator. Create a vision board or use visualization techniques to vividly imagine yourself successfully reaching your goals. Engage your senses and experience the emotions associated with your desired achievements. Visualizing your future success helps to reinforce your motivation, enhance your belief in what is possible, and keep your focus unwavering.

Another effective strategy is to cultivate a positive and supportive environment. Surround yourself with individuals who uplift and inspire you, whether they are friends, mentors, or like-minded peers. Share your goals and aspirations with them, and seek their encouragement and support. Their belief in your abilities and their positive energy can significantly boost your motivation, especially during challenging times.

Regularly revisiting your progress and celebrating your achievements is also vital for maintaining motivation. Acknowledge and appreciate the progress you've made, no matter how small. Celebrate your victories, however insignificant they may seem, as they signify that you are moving forward. Recognize the effort and dedication you've put in, and let it fuel your motivation to keep going.

By clarifying your purpose, setting meaningful goals, visualizing success, cultivating a positive environment, embracing a growth mindset, celebrating achievements, and practicing self-care, you can fuel your drive and stay motivated even in the face of challenges. These strategies will support you in sustaining the momentum and enthusiasm needed to continue your journey towards success and fulfillment.

CONCLUSION

As we reach the conclusion of "The Power of a First Step: Ignite Your Journey to Success and Fulfillment," it is essential to reflect on the transformative journey we have embarked upon. Throughout this book, we have explored the profound impact of taking that initial step towards our dreams and aspirations. We have delved into the strategies, mindsets, and actions necessary to navigate obstacles, overcome self-doubt, and maintain unwavering motivation. Now, as we wrap up this empowering journey, let us embrace the key lessons and insights that will guide us towards a life of fulfillment and success.

First and foremost, we have learned that the power of a first step lies not only in its significance but also in its ability to set in motion a chain of events that can shape our destiny. By summoning the courage to take that initial leap, we ignite a spark within ourselves, opening up a world of possibilities and opportunities. Each subsequent step becomes an affirmation of our commitment to realizing our dreams, propelling us forward on our unique path.

Throughout this book, we have encountered the importance of self-belief, resilience, and perseverance. We have discovered the transformative impact of embracing change, overcoming fear, and redefining failure. We have learned to cultivate a growth mindset, harness the power of positive thinking, and develop effective goal-setting strategies. These insights, when applied in our lives, empower us to conquer obstacles, stay focused, and consistently take action towards our goals.

Moreover, we have recognized that the journey to success and fulfillment is not a solitary one. It is enriched by the support and encouragement of those around us, who uplift and inspire us to reach greater heights. Building a network of like-minded individuals, mentors, and guides can provide valuable insights, guidance, and accountability, fueling our progress and propelling us towards our aspirations.

As we conclude this book, let us embrace the notion that fulfillment and success are not just destinations but a way of life. It is not solely about achieving external markers of success but also about experiencing a deep sense of purpose, joy, and fulfillment along the way. It is about aligning our actions with our values, nurturing our passions, and making a positive impact on the world around us.

Remember that the journey to success and fulfillment is not without its challenges. It may require us to step out of our comfort zones, face adversity, and make sacrifices. However, armed with the wisdom and insights gained from this book, we possess the tools and mindset to overcome any obstacle that comes our way. We have the power to transform setbacks into stepping stones, setbacks into opportunities, and fear into fuel for growth.

As you embark on your own journey towards success and fulfillment, carry with you the lessons, strategies, and inspiration garnered from "The Power of a First Step." Embrace the power of decisive action, cultivate a resilient mindset, and maintain unwavering motivation. Set clear goals, surround yourself with a supportive community, and practice self-care along the way.

Embrace each step of your journey with gratitude, curiosity, and a spirit of adventure. Embrace the uncertainty and the unknown, for within them lies the potential for extraordinary growth and discovery. And most importantly, remember that your journey is unique to you. Embrace your individuality, celebrate your progress, and savor the moments of joy and fulfillment that come along the way.

May "The Power of a First Step" serve as a guiding light as you navigate the twists and turns of your path. May it remind you of your inner strength, resilience, and limitless potential. Embrace the journey, embrace your power, and embrace a life filled with fulfillment and success.

APPENDIX

In this appendix of "The Power of a First Step: Ignite Your Journey to Success and Fulfillment," we provide you with a collection of actionable exercises and reflection questions. These exercises are designed to deepen your understanding, strengthen your commitment, and provide practical tools for applying the concepts discussed throughout the book. By engaging with these exercises, you can actively integrate the principles into your life and propel yourself further on your path to success and fulfillment. Take the time to explore each exercise and reflect on the questions to gain valuable insights and develop a personalized action plan.

1. *Goal Setting Exercise:*

- Define your short-term and long-term goals.

- Break down each goal into specific, measurable, attainable, relevant, and time-bound (SMART) objectives.

- Identify potential obstacles and develop strategies to overcome them.

- Set deadlines for each milestone and create a timeline for achieving your goals.

2. *Vision Board Creation:*

- Gather images, quotes, and symbols that represent your aspirations and desired outcomes.

- Create a vision board by arranging these visuals on a board or in a digital format.

- Display your vision board in a prominent place where you can see it daily.

- Reflect on your vision board regularly and visualize yourself living your desired future.

3. *Self-Reflection:*

- Take time to reflect on your values, passions, and purpose in life.

- Consider how your goals align with your core values and contribute to your overall sense of fulfillment.

- Reflect on past experiences that have

brought you joy, growth, and a sense of accomplishment.

- Identify patterns and themes that emerge from your reflections and use them as guidance in shaping your journey.

4. *Overcoming Fear and Self-Doubt:*

- List your fears and self-limiting beliefs that may be holding you back.
- Challenge each fear and belief by gathering evidence that contradicts them.
- Develop affirmations or positive statements to counteract negative self-talk.
- Take small steps outside of your comfort zone to gradually build confidence and overcome fears.

5. *Action Plan Development:*

- Review your goals and milestones.
- Break down each milestone into actionable steps.
- Assign deadlines to each step and prioritize them based on importance and urgency.
- Create a written action plan that outlines your steps and timelines.

6. *Gratitude Practice:*

- Start a gratitude journal and write down

three things you are grateful for each day.

- Take time to express gratitude to others who have supported you on your journey.

- Reflect on the positive aspects of each step you have taken and acknowledge the progress you have made.

7. Accountability Partnership:

- Identify a trusted friend, mentor, or accountability partner who can support you on your journey.

- Share your goals, progress, and challenges with your accountability partner.

- Schedule regular check-ins or meetings to review your progress and provide mutual support.

Reflection Questions:

- What is your biggest take away from this book, and how will you apply it to your life?

- What fears or self-doubts have been holding you back, and how can you overcome them?

- How can you incorporate the strategies discussed in this book into your daily routine?

- What steps will you take to cultivate discipline, resilience, and consistency in pursuing your goals?

- How will you leverage setbacks and failures as opportunities for growth and learning?

- How can you create a supportive environment and surround yourself with like-minded individuals?

- What self-care practices will you prioritize to maintain your motivation and well-being?

- How will you hold yourself accountable for taking consistent action towards your goals?

- What adjustments or refinements will you make to your action plan as you progress on your journey?

Remember, the exercises and reflection questions in this appendix are meant to guide and inspire you. Embrace them with an open mind and commit to taking meaningful action. Regularly revisit these exercises and questions to track your progress, make adjustments, and ensure that you stay aligned with your vision and purpose. By engaging wholeheartedly with these activities, you will harness the full potential of "The Power of a First Step" and ignite your journey to success and fulfillment.

ABOUT THE AUTHOR

Johnathan Rivers is a fervent advocate for personal growth and self-discovery, having undergone his own transformative journey. Deeply acquainted with the profound impact of initiating change, Johnathan encourages and inspires others to embark on their unique paths of self-discovery and growth.

Facing various challenges throughout his life, one of Johnathan's significant hurdles was summoning the courage to begin writing his book. Wrestling with self-doubt and the fear of failure, he, like many aspiring authors, confronted daunting obstacles. Nevertheless, fueled by determination and a belief in the significance of his message, Johnathan overcame these barriers and delved into the writing process.

This personal struggle to take the first step profoundly shaped Johnathan's understanding of its transformative power. He personally experienced how embracing the initial leap into the unknown opens up a realm of self-discovery, growth, and fulfillment. In his book, Johnathan shares his journey and the invaluable lessons he learned, offering readers insights into the process of self-discovery and growth that unfolds when mustering the courage to take that first step.

Readers are encouraged through Johnathan's words to embark on their own paths of self-discovery, understanding that each step holds the potential for personal transformation. Whether pursuing long-held dreams, overcoming fears, or seeking purpose and fulfillment, Johnathan believes the first step is the catalyst that sets everything in motion.

Guiding readers through the self-discovery journey with captivating storytelling, Johnathan's unwavering belief in the power of the first step serves as a beacon of inspiration. It reminds readers that genuine growth and self-discovery lie just beyond the edge of their comfort zones.

A former Electrical Engineer who successfully transitioned to Mechanical Engineering, Johnathan Rivers passionately advocates for personal growth. He understands the immense potential within each individual, firmly believing that taking the first step is not only the key to self-discovery but also a gateway to unlocking one's true potential and living a purposeful and fulfilling life.

Johnathan eagerly anticipates accompanying readers on their transformative journeys of self-discovery and growth.

www.ingramcontent.com/pod-product-compliance
Lightning Source LLC
Chambersburg PA
CBHW052037150726
48002CB00002B/643